The Simple Art of

Convection Cooking

source. It is also the setting to use for roasting, multirack baking, and cooking complete meals where the airflow is impeded by the dishes. When convection-roasting meats and poultry, place the food on a V-shaped roasting rack set in a roasting pan. This will allow air to circulate around the roast, lock in the juices, and give it a beautiful brown exterior, while shortening the cooking time in most cases.

Note: Any recipe that uses the Convection Bake setting will turn out even better if cooked on the True or Pure Convection setting. We use Convection Bake throughout this book as the standard setting because not all ovens have the True or Pure Convection setting.

EQUIPMENT BASICS

Here are a few special pieces of equipment that will maximize your oven's performance.

Baking Sheets: For foods that release liquid, choose medium-gauge aluminum pans with a rim, also known as jelly-roll pans or commercial half-sheet pans. They will stay flat during baking and conduct heat evenly. For foods such as cookies, use regular rimless baking sheets, but not insulated ones, which can slow the browning process.

Heavy Roasting Pan: For meats and poultry, as well as for some vegetables. Choose a standard roasting pan with straight, relatively shallow sides (not the deep turkey roaster with a lid).

V-shaped Roasting Rack: A rack that fits inside the roasting pan ensures that meat and poultry are seared all over, delivering a crisp outside and a juicy, tender inside.

Instant-read Thermometer: This inexpensive device is a must for any home cook who wants perfect results every time. When using an instant-read thermometer, insert it in the thickest part of the food, not touching bone. For poultry, insert the thermometer into the thickest part of the thigh, between the body and the leg.

CONVERTING COOKING TIMES FOR NONCONVECTION RECIPES

The recipes in this book were specifically designed and tested for convection cooking, but it is easy to convert your old recipes so you can make the most of your oven. You will rarely need to adjust the temperature of the oven unless you are cooking desserts; when cooking most desserts reduce the temperature by 25 degrees. As for cooking time, this changes very little for foods that cook in less than 30 minutes. For foods that take 30 minutes or more, the cooking time should be reduced by about 25 percent. The bigger the food, the faster it will cook; this makes a marked difference in foods such as turkeys and prime ribs. Use your instant-read thermometer to gauge doneness.

The only time we don't use the convection mode is with delicate dishes such as custards, where browning is unwanted, or when the convection air won't touch the food, such as cheesecakes in a water bath or a turkey in a covered roaster. With few exceptions, we use the convection mode for most baked, broiled, and grilled foods as well as for steamed and braised ones, and if you follow the above simple rules, you can do the same.

The Simple Art of Convection Cooking will allow you to use the convection mode on your oven with confidence. Once you begin using the recipes in this book, you will understand the many advantages this kind of cooking offers. As we discovered in our first restaurant kitchen, convection cooking not only saves time and energy, it results in better food, from appetizers to desserts. Now that this kind of cooking is widely available for home cooks, we hope you will enjoy the benefits that professional cooks have known for years.

For example, you'll find that roasting chicken on the Convection Bake setting renders the fat faster, yielding a crisp-skinned, juicy chicken in under one hour. In fact, most dishes you'd normally roast for hours take only 75 percent of the time when baked in the convection oven mode.

One of our favorite convection-baked foods is pizza: The convection mode yields pizzas with a restaurant-quality crust in less than 15 minutes. And convection baking is unmatched for baked goods; cakes, muffins, and pastries not only rise faster and higher in a convection oven, they come out golden brown and even in color every time. And the convection mode is perfect when you want to bake in quantity: You can cook five or six racks of baked goods at one time without having to rotate the pans.

CONVECTION SYSTEMS

There are two basic types of convection-oven systems. The first kind has a top element, a bottom element, and a fan that moves the air throughout the oven. The second type of system, usually found in higher-end ovens, includes an additional element in the back of the oven surrounding the fan, which circulates the heated air inside the oven cavity. Some companies term this setting simply Convection, or it may be called Pure Convection or True Convection. This back element forces hot air horizontally through the oven racks, which is a boon when cooking food on multiple racks. Instead of being impeded by the quantity and density of the food, the hot air is forced around the baked goods to cook them evenly. This capability allows food to be cooked on the lowest rack of the oven without burning, because the bottom element does not turn on during this setting.

Some high-end ovens have another feature: a filtering system that is activated in convection mode. While a small part of an oven's operation, this feature is helpful because it prevents the transfer of odor from one dish to another.

This means that you can cook several different kinds of dishes—even an entire meal—at one time without any dish taking on the flavors of its neighbor. A secondary benefit of the filtering system is that it helps the oven to operate more cleanly.

CONVECTION SETTINGS

Every oven with the convection capability has two basic settings, Convection Bake and Convection Broil, while higher-end ovens have the third basic setting, Convection, (also called True Convection or Pure Convection). Your oven may have even more convection settings; if so, consult your oven manual to learn how to use these settings.

Convection Bake: This setting is best for foods that need bottom heat in order to cook properly, yet can also benefit from the even heat produced through convection. This includes thick, dense dishes such as lasagnas and gratins, pies, and loaf breads, as well as dishes where a crisp bottom crust is desirable, such as pizzas and breads baked on a baking stone.

Convection Broil: Use this setting to broil fish, meats, poultry, and vegetables, and to brown foods such as garlic bread and gratins. Convection Broil cooks food at a hotter temperature than standard broiling, because the fan pushes heat down from the top of the oven. The fan-blown hot air helps to seal the exterior of foods quickly and cook them faster than with a conventional broiler, while the upper heating element caramelizes the top of the food at the same time. For best results, center the broiler pan under the heating element.

Convection (also known as True, or Pure, Convection): Once the oven is preheated, this convection setting uses a rear heating element rather than a top or bottom one, which enables better air circulation around pans and baking sheets. Foods that are relatively light in texture or thin in depth, such as soufflés, cakes, cookies, and pastries, greatly benefit from this more centralized heat

INTRODUCTION

Twenty years ago, when my husband, John, and I first stepped into a commercial kitchen, the convection oven was the star of every restaurant work space. A giant stainless-steel monster, it cooked vast quantities of vegetables, roasts, and baked goods. **Working with a convection oven for the first time in our careers, we found that it was an amazing time-saver.** With a conventional restaurant oven, you could cook only two sheet pans of food, and during the process you had to rotate the pans to allow for even browning. The commercial convection oven changed all that, combining a greatly enlarged oven space with the ability to brown foods evenly.

The concept behind the convection oven is simple: The heat in a conventional oven is essentially uneven, because the air is hottest near the oven's heating element and cooler elsewhere, and this uneven temperature results in uneven browning and cooking. The convection oven is equipped with a fan that circulates the hot air; this equalizes the hot and cold spots. As a result, food cooks and browns more evenly in a shorter period of time and usually at a lower temperature, and therefore the oven uses less energy.

The convection oven was invented in the sixties and soon became popular in bakeries and restaurants. Chefs and bakers quickly learned to appreciate the benefits of convection cooking, and the ovens became a staple in most commercial kitchens. Because commercial convection ovens were bulky and expensive, however, this kind of cooking did not become available to home cooks until the last few years, when home ovens were developed to offer both conventional and convection baking modes.

Today, just about every oven sold for the home kitchen has the convection option. (Small combination convection, toaster, and broiler ovens are also available.) The dedicated convection oven of the professional chef has been transformed into an oven for the home cook that allows both traditional and convection baking, roasting, and broiling. Home cooks who have no experience with this kind of cooking may be intimidated and confused by the convection mode.

As the chef/owners of Caprial's Bistro in Portland, Oregon, where we also run a cooking school (Caprial and John's Kitchen), we have learned to treasure the many advantages of convection cooking. But time and time again while we were teaching our classes, we found that our students would say, "Help me—how do I use my convection oven?" Many of our students had never even turned on the convection mode.

After years of hearing these cries for help, we decided that it was time to demystify convection ovens. Time-saving and energy-saving, convection cooking is superior to the conventional oven mode, and it is not difficult to learn. With very little change in your everyday cooking habits, you will be rewarded with amazing results from your oven.

You will find that some foods cook much better using the convection mode. Roasted vegetables, for example, especially potatoes, don't even need to be stirred or turned; they come out of the oven golden brown and crunchy, because the sugars in vegetables caramelize faster in a convection oven, yielding better flavor and texture. Another star of the convection oven is poultry.

CONTENTS

ACKNOWLEDGMENTS

Thanks to everyone at Dacor for making such a great product.
Thanks to Kevin Toyama at Chronicle Books for being so patient with us.
Thanks to our family, who always supports us.

ISBN-10: 0-8118-5882-0
ISBN-13: 978-0-8118-5882-3

Design: Empire Design Studio
Photo Assistants: Sara Johnson Loehmann, Gene Lee, and Ian Stout
Stylist: Elisabet der Nederlanden
Manufactured in China.

10 9 8 7 6 5 4 3 2 1

Chronicle Books LLC
680 Second Street
San Francisco, California 94107

www.chroniclebooks.com

The Simple Art of

Convection Cooking

by Caprial *and* John Pence

Photographs by Noel Barnhurst

CHRONICLE BOOKS

SAN FRANCISCO

AT HOME AND AT RESTAURANTS, WE SOMETIMES CREATE A WHOLE MEAL FROM JUST APPETIZERS. THIS CHAPTER FEATURES APPETIZERS THAT ARE TASTY BUT NOT TOO TIME-CONSUMING TO MAKE. **YOU WANT TO DAZZLE YOUR GUESTS WITH THEIR FIRST BITES OF FOOD, BUT YOU DON'T WANT THE PREPARATIONS TO TAKE ALL DAY.**

APPETIZERS

Oven-Steamed Mussels
with Lime-Ginger Butter

Steaming mussels in a hot oven is so easy; in about 20 minutes you have a wonderful appetizer, or a simple dinner to serve with bread and green salad.

Serves 4 as an appetizer, 2 as an entree

2 ½ pounds **mussels**, scrubbed and debearded

1 tablespoon minced fresh **ginger**

2 cloves **garlic**, minced

Grated zest and juice of 2 **limes**

¼ cup **dry white wine**

1 teaspoon minced fresh **cilantro** or **basil**

2 tablespoons unsalted **butter**

2 teaspoons **fish sauce**

Pinch of **red pepper flakes**

Salt to taste

Preheat the oven to 450°F on Convection Bake. In a large ovenproof sauté pan or skillet, combine all of the ingredients. Cover and bake in the oven for 8 minutes. Stir well. Re-cover and bake just until the mussels open, 8 to 10 minutes longer. Remove from the oven. Discard any mussels that have not opened. Divide the mussels among 4 bowls. Taste the broth for salt. Ladle the broth over the mussels and serve.

Oven-Roasted Clams
with Bacon *and* Saffron

During the summer months, we take advantage of our garden by adding diced fresh tomatoes to the broth for this dish. Occasionally, we finish it with toasted ground almonds to give it a Spanish flair.

Serves 4 as an appetizer, 2 as an entree

4 slices **bacon**, diced

½ **onion**, finely chopped

3 cloves **garlic**, minced

2 ½ pounds **clams**, scrubbed

¼ cup **dry white wine**

Pinch of **saffron threads**

2 tablespoons unsalted **butter**

1 tablespoon minced fresh **flat-leaf parsley**

Salt and freshly ground **pepper** to taste

Preheat the oven to 450°F on Convection Bake. In a large ovenproof sauté pan or skillet, combine the bacon and onion. Roast in the oven, stirring once or twice, until the bacon is crisp, 4 to 5 minutes. Add the garlic, clams, wine, saffron, and butter. Cover and roast in the oven for 10 minutes. Stir well.

Re-cover and roast until the clams have opened, about 10 minutes. Remove from the oven. Discard any clams that have not opened. Add the parsley. Divide the clams among 4 bowls. Season the broth with salt and pepper and ladle over the clams. Serve.

Broiled Oysters
with Lemon-Herb Pesto

The pesto in this recipe is **so versatile** that you can toss it with pasta or smear it on top of a New York steak. If you decide to substitute different herbs in the recipe, stay with soft-leafed annuals such as basil and fennel. **Serves 6**

LEMON-HERB PESTO

1 cup fresh **flat-leaf parsley leaves**

½ cup fresh **tarragon leaves**

½ cup fresh **dill sprigs**

3 cloves **garlic**

½ cup (2 ounces) grated **Parmesan cheese**

⅓ cup **pine nuts**, toasted (see page 151)

Grated zest of 2 **lemons**

⅓ cup extra-virgin **olive oil**

Pinch of **red pepper flakes**

Salt and freshly ground **pepper** to taste

2 dozen **oysters** on the half shell

Rock salt for serving

Preheat the oven on high on Convection Broil. To make the pesto: In a food processor, puree the parsley, tarragon, dill, and garlic until smooth. Add the cheese, pine nuts, and lemon zest and process until smooth. With the machine running, gradually add the olive oil. Add the pepper flakes, salt, and pepper. Set aside.

Place the oysters on a sided baking sheet. Top each oyster with 1 teaspoon pesto. Place under the broiler about 4 inches from the heat source and broil until golden brown, about 3 minutes. Remove and place on a tray lined with rock salt. Serve warm.

Orange-Glazed Cocktail Ribs

Whenever John and I serve these ribs at our house, they are a big hit. We adjust the spice in the glaze depending on who's coming to dinner. **Make these the day ahead and heat them gently just before serving** to ease your workload. **Serves 6**

3 pounds **spareribs**, cut in half lengthwise to form 6 sections

Salt and freshly ground **pepper** to taste

ORANGE GLAZE

½ cup **honey**

¼ cup **mirin wine**

2 teaspoons minced fresh **ginger**

2 cloves **garlic**, minced

2 heaping tablespoons **frozen orange juice concentrate**

Grated zest and juice of 1 **orange**

2 teaspoons **Dijon mustard**

1 teaspoon **chili sauce**, such as sriracha

Salt to taste

Preheat the oven to 250°F on Convection Bake. In a roasting pan, place as many of the ribs as will fit without overcrowding. Use two pans if needed. Season well with salt and pepper. Add about ½ cup of water to each pan. Cover with aluminum foil. Bake in the oven for 1 hour.

While the ribs are baking, make the glaze: In a medium bowl, combine all of the ingredients and mix well. Set aside.

Remove the foil and increase the oven temperature to 300°F. Brush the ribs well with the glaze and bake, brushing with the glaze every 10 to 15 minutes, until tender, about 1 more hour. Cut into individual ribs, place on a platter, and serve.

Mediterranean Chicken Wings

My mom is the queen of chicken wings in our family, but we think this recipe is up to her standards. We also like to **use this marinade on whole chicken, pork roast, and even flank steak.**

Serves 4

2 pounds **chicken wings**

4 cloves **garlic**, minced

Grated zest and juice of 3 **lemons**

½ cup extra-virgin **olive oil**

1 teaspoon **sweet paprika**

½ teaspoon **red pepper flakes**

½ teaspoon ground **cumin**

Salt to taste

Put the chicken wings in a large resealable plastic bag. Add all of the remaining ingredients. Seal the bag and rotate it to coat the wings. Refrigerate for 4 to 6 hours.

Preheat the oven to 375°F on Convection Bake. Spread the chicken wings in a roasting pan and pour the marinade over. Bake in the oven for 20 minutes, then stir well. Bake for another 25 minutes, or until tender and golden brown. Remove from the oven, place on a large platter, and serve.

Spicy Ginger Chicken Satay

Satay is a **perfect appetizer for a large group**; you can make the skewers ahead of time, and they just take minutes to cook. If you have vegetarians coming to the party, skewer a selection of vegetables and use the same marinade. **Makes 12 skewers**

12 ounces **boneless, skinless chicken breasts**

¼ cup **honey**

1 tablespoon grated fresh **ginger**

3 cloves garlic, minced

½ teaspoon **red pepper flakes**

2 tablespoons **soy sauce**

DIPPING SAUCE

1 cup **Thai sweet chili sauce**

Grated zest and juice of 2 **limes**

1 tablespoon **soy sauce**

With a meat mallet or the bottom of a saucepan, pound the chicken breasts to flatten them to an even thickness. Cut into 12 lengthwise strips and set aside. In a small bowl, whisk the honey, ginger, garlic, pepper flakes, and soy sauce together. Pour over the chicken and toss well to coat. Cover and refrigerate for at least 30 minutes or up to 1 hour. Meanwhile, soak 12 wooden skewers in water.

To make the sauce: In a small bowl, combine all the ingredients and whisk until smooth. Set aside.

Preheat the oven on high on Convection Broil. Thread the chicken strips onto the skewers. Place on a broiler pan in a single layer. Place under the broiler about 4 inches from the heat source and cook for about 2 minutes on each side, or just until opaque throughout. Remove from the oven and serve hot, with the dipping sauce alongside.

Broiled Artichokes
with Honey-Basil Dressing

We first cooked these artichokes on the grill, but **the broiler caramelizes the dressing** even better. There is no need for a dipping sauce because of the dressing.

Serves 4

4 **artichokes**, trimmed
(see page 151)

¼ cup **Champagne vinegar**

3 cloves **garlic**, minced

1 small **shallot**, minced

1 tablespoon **Dijon mustard**

3 tablespoons **honey**

1 tablespoon minced
fresh **basil**

¾ cup extra-virgin **olive oil**

Salt and freshly ground
pepper to taste

In a large pot of boiling water, cook the artichokes until tender, about 25 minutes. Drain and let cool. Using a teaspoon, remove the choke with a small paring knife and scoop any remaining choke with a spoon. Place the artichokes in a large bowl and set aside.

In a small bowl, whisk the vinegar, garlic, shallot, mustard, honey, and basil together until smooth. Gradually whisk in the olive oil until smooth. Season with salt and pepper. Pour over the artichokes and toss well. Let stand at room temperature for about 30 minutes.

Preheat the oven on high on Convection Broil. Remove the artichokes from the marinade, reserving the marinade. Place on a broiler pan in a single layer, cut side up. Place under the broiler about 4 inches from the heat source and broil for 3 minutes, or until the artichokes start to brown. Remove from the oven and return to the marinade. Toss to coat. Place on a large platter and serve.

Bruschetta
with Caramelized Onions *and* Fromage Blanc

We often teach our students to caramelize onions on the stove top, **but the oven is so much easier**, and the onions tend to brown more evenly and taste better. Make extra caramelized onions to toss with pasta or add to soup.

Makes 12 toasts; serves 4

2 **yellow onions**, cut into julienne

2 teaspoons minced fresh **thyme**

1 tablespoon extra-virgin **olive oil**

Salt and freshly ground **pepper** to taste

2 cloves **garlic**, minced

3/4 cup **fromage blanc cheese**

12 **crostini** (page 149)

Preheat the oven to 425°F on Convection Bake. Place a sided baking sheet in the oven to preheat for about 10 minutes. In a medium bowl, combine the onions, thyme, olive oil, salt, and pepper. Toss well and spread on the preheated pan. Bake in the oven until the onions are golden brown and tender, about 25 minutes. Remove from the oven and stir in the garlic.

Spread each of the crostini with about 1 tablespoon of the fromage blanc, then top with a heaping tablespoon of the warm onion mixture. Serve at room temperature.

Bruschetta
with Roasted Tomatoes, Eggplant, *and* Capers

Preheating the pan is important to this recipe; **it helps to caramelize the eggplant**, which enhances the flavor of the bruschetta. As with all tomato-based recipes, use ripe tomatoes in season. **Makes 12 toasts; serves 4**

2 **tomatoes**, halved, seeded, and diced

1 small **eggplant**, diced

2 tablespoons extra-virgin **olive oil**

Salt and freshly ground **pepper** to taste

2 cloves **garlic**, minced

2 tablespoons good-quality **balsamic vinegar**

2 teaspoons minced **capers**

1 tablespoon minced fresh **basil**

12 **crostini** (page 149)

⅓ cup shaved **Parmesan cheese**

Preheat the oven to 425°F on Convection Bake. Place a sided baking sheet in the oven to preheat for about 10 minutes. In a medium bowl, combine the tomatoes, eggplant, olive oil, salt, and pepper. Toss well to coat.

Spread the tomato mixture on the preheated pan and roast in the oven until the eggplant is browned and tender, about 20 minutes. Remove from the oven and scrape into a medium bowl. Add the garlic, vinegar, capers, basil, and salt and pepper to taste; mix well.

Top each of the crostini with a heaping tablespoon of the eggplant mixture and garnish with the shaved cheese. Serve warm or at room temperature.

The Simple Art of Convection Cooking

Warm Artichoke Dip

My best friend, Molly, calls this dip addictive; we love it because it can be made one day ahead and popped under the broiler just before serving. **Serves 4**

½ cup **dry white wine**

2 cloves **garlic**, minced

1 cup **heavy cream**

1 cup (8 ounces) **cream cheese**

1 tablespoon **Dijon mustard**

1 tablespoon minced fresh **basil**

½ teaspoon **Worcestershire sauce**

¼ cup grated **Parmesan cheese**

1 tablespoon **cayenne sauce**

One 14½-ounce can **artichoke bottoms**, drained and diced

Salt and freshly ground **pepper** to taste

1 cup fresh **bread crumbs**

Crostini, pita chips, or **baguette slices** for serving

Preheat the oven on high on Convection Broil. In a large saucepan, combine the wine and garlic. Cook over high heat to reduce to about ¼ cup. Add the cream and cook over high heat until the cream mixture is reduced by half and coats the back of a spoon, 4 to 5 minutes. Reduce the heat to medium and stir in the cream cheese and mustard until smooth. Add the basil, Worcestershire sauce, Parmesan cheese, cayenne sauce, and artichokes and mix well. Season with salt and pepper.

Pour the dip into an ovenproof bowl or 8-cup soufflé dish. Top with the bread crumbs. Place under the broiler about 4 inches from the heat source and broil until golden brown, 3 to 4 minutes. Remove from the oven, place on a trivet, and serve with crostini, pita chips, or baguette slices for dipping.

Roasted Red Pepper Dip

Greek yogurt, used in this recipe, is thicker and creamier than American yogurt. If you can't find Greek yogurt in your area, try substituting sour cream and a bit of heavy cream. **This dip also works well as a sauce** for grilled fish or a New York steak.

Makes about 2 cups; serves 4

4 large **red bell peppers**, roasted and peeled (see page 151)

1 **jalapeno chili**, roasted and peeled (see page 151)

3 cloves **garlic**, minced

1 cup **Greek yogurt**

1 teaspoon **sweet Spanish smoked paprika** (pimentón)

2 teaspoons minced fresh **flat-leaf parsley**

1 teaspoon minced fresh **oregano**

Salt and freshly ground **pepper** to taste

Pita chips for serving

In a food processor, puree the peppers, chili, and garlic. Add the yogurt, paprika, and herbs and pulse to mix. Season with salt and pepper. Serve at room temperature, with pita chips for dipping.

ON A WET WINTER EVENING, **SOUP IS ONE OF THE MOST COMFORTING FOODS YOU CAN SERVE** YOUR GUESTS. **SALADS ARE A YEAR-ROUND DISH** AT OUR HOUSE; IN THE SUMMER THEY ARE LIGHTER, AND WE MAY SERVE THEM AS THE ENTREE, WHILE IN WINTER THEY ARE MORE SUBSTANTIAL AND ARE OFTEN SERVED WITH A SAVORY SOUP.

SOUPS & SALADS

Roasted Chili and Tomato Soup

Ancho chilies, used in this soup, **are very mild, with a rich chocolate flavor.** If you would like a spicier soup, add a couple of diced jalapenos to the recipe. We often make this dish more substantial by adding grilled prawns or leftover roast chicken. **Serves 4**

8 **tomatoes**, halved and seeded

2 **ancho chilies**

6 cloves **garlic**

½ cup extra-virgin **olive oil**

2 teaspoons ground **cumin**

2 teaspoons dried **oregano**

2 teaspoons minced fresh **cilantro**

4 cups **chicken** or **vegetable stock**

Salt and freshly ground **pepper** to taste

1 **avocado**, pitted, peeled, and diced

½ cup **sour cream**

Preheat the oven to 425°F on Convection Bake. In a large roasting pan, combine the tomatoes, chilies, garlic, and olive oil. Toss to coat. Roast in the oven until the tomatoes are very soft and browned, 30 to 35 minutes. Transfer the mixture to a large saucepan and add the cumin, oregano, cilantro, and stock. Bring to a boil, reduce the heat, and simmer for 15 minutes.

In a blender, carefully puree the soup, in batches if necessary, then strain through a sieve back into the saucepan. Season with salt and pepper. Reheat the soup. Serve hot, garnished with avocado and a dollop of sour cream.

Roasted Root Vegetable Soup

We love to take advantage of the produce of the season, and this soup is a prime example. If another root vegetable catches your eye, by all means add it to the soup. A half ounce of dried mushrooms added to the soup with the stock lends a warm, earthy flavor. **Serves 4**

1 small **onion**, diced

2 **parsnips**, peeled and diced

2 **carrots**, peeled and diced

1 small **celeriac** (celery root), peeled and diced

1 small bulb **fennel**, trimmed and diced

4 cloves **garlic**

¼ cup extra-virgin **olive oil**

Salt and freshly ground **pepper** to taste

2 teaspoons minced fresh **thyme**

1 teaspoon minced fresh **sage**

4 cups **vegetable** or **chicken stock**

Preheat the oven to 425°F on Convection Bake. Place a large roasting pan in the oven to preheat for about 15 minutes. In a large bowl, combine the onion, parsnips, carrots, celeriac, fennel, garlic, olive oil, salt, and pepper. Toss well to coat. Spread the vegetables on the preheated pan. Roast in the oven for about 30 minutes, or until golden brown and tender.

Scrape the vegetables into a large stockpot. Add the fresh herbs and stock. Bring to a boil over high heat, then reduce the heat to a simmer and cook for about 20 minutes to reduce and thicken the liquid. In a blender, carefully puree the soup, in batches if necessary. Reheat the soup before serving, if desired. Taste and adjust the seasoning. Serve.

Spicy Black Bean Soup

You can use canned black beans to shorten the cooking time of this soup, but if you have time, making your own is always a good idea. **We love to make a double batch of this soup** and freeze half for a night when we are too tired to cook.

Serves 4

1 small **onion**, diced

2 stalks **celery**, diced

1 small **red bell pepper**, seeded, deribbed, and diced

2 small **jalapeno chilies**, seeded and diced

2 tablespoons extra-virgin **olive oil**

3 cloves **garlic**, minced

4 cups **cooked black beans**

5 cups **chicken stock**

1 cup canned **diced tomatoes**

1 small **ham hock**

2 teaspoons ground **cumin**

2 teaspoons **chili powder**

2 teaspoons **ancho chili powder**

2 teaspoons minced fresh **cilantro**

Salt and freshly ground **pepper** to taste

⅓ cup **sour cream**

Preheat a large Dutch oven in the oven for about 20 minutes. In a medium bowl, combine the onion, celery, bell pepper, chili, and olive oil. Toss to coat. Add the onion mixture and garlic to the hot Dutch oven and cook, reaching in to stir occasionally, for about 5 minutes or until tender. Add the beans, stock, tomatoes, and ham hock. Cover and cook for about 45 minutes, or until the stock is very flavorful. Place the soup on the stove top over medium heat to keep the soup warm. Add the spices, cilantro, salt, and pepper. Serve with a dollop of sour cream.

Cream of Roasted Fennel Soup

This creamy fennel soup is so satisfying on a chilly fall night—it's the perfect beginning to a dinner party or the entree for a simple supper. **Parsnips would be a great addition to this soup,** as they add just a bit of sweetness.

Serves 4 as a first course, 2 to 3 as an entree

3 large **fennel bulbs**, trimmed (reserve fronds) and chopped

1 small **celeriac** (celery root), peeled and chopped

1 **onion**, chopped

2 tablespoons extra-virgin **olive oil**

Salt and freshly ground **pepper** to taste

3 cloves **garlic**, minced

1 cup **dry sherry**

4 cups **chicken** or **vegetable stock**

½ cup **heavy cream**

Preheat the oven to 425°F on Convection Bake. Place a roasting pan in the oven to preheat for about 10 minutes. In a large bowl, combine the chopped fennel, celeriac, onion, olive oil, salt, and pepper. Spread on the preheated pan and roast in the oven for about 30 minutes, or until the vegetables are very tender and caramelized. Scrape the vegetable mixture into a large saucepan. Add the garlic and sherry, bring to a boil over high heat, and cook to reduce the liquid by half, 3 to 4 minutes.

Add the stock and cook for about 15 minutes to reduce and thicken the liquid.

In a blender, carefully puree the soup, in batches if necessary. Pass through a sieve if you would like the soup smoother. Return to the saucepan. Mince enough of the reserved fennel fronds to yield 1 tablespoon. Add the cream and fennel fronds and heat briefly. Taste and adjust the seasoning. Serve.

Roasted Beet Salad
with Fontina *and* Hazelnuts

Our roasted beet salad sells so well at the Bistro that we decided to include a recipe on how to make it at home. **Roasted beets also make a nice side dish** to serve with roasted pork or chicken. **Serves 4**

4 beets, peeled and diced

2 tablespoons extra-virgin **olive oil**, plus ½ cup

Salt and freshly ground **pepper** to taste

2 tablespoons **red wine vinegar**

1 teaspoon **Dijon mustard**

2 cloves **garlic**, minced

⅔ cup (3 ounces) shredded **fontina cheese**

½ cup **hazelnuts**, toasted, skinned (see page 151), and chopped

Preheat the oven to 425°F on Convection Bake. In a medium bowl, combine the beets, the 2 tablespoons olive oil, the salt, and pepper. Toss to coat. Spread on a baking sheet in one layer. Roast in the oven for about 15 minutes, or until tender.

While the beets are roasting, make the dressing: In a small bowl, combine the vinegar, mustard, and garlic. Whisk until smooth. Gradually whisk in the ½ cup olive oil until smooth. Season with salt and pepper to taste.

Divide the warm beets among 4 plates and drizzle with the dressing. Top with the cheese and hazelnuts. Serve.

Roasted Cherry Tomato Salad
with Shaved Parmesan

Roasting the cherry tomatoes brings out their sweet flavor. Use a variety of colors of tomatoes to make the salad visually striking. **Serves 4**

4 cups ripe **cherry tomatoes**

2 tablespoons extra-virgin **olive oil**

2 tablespoons good-quality **balsamic vinegar**

2 cloves **garlic**, minced

1 tablespoon minced fresh **basil**

2/3 cup shaved **Parmesan cheese**

Salt and **cracked pepper** to taste

Preheat the oven to 425°F on Convection Bake. Place a roasting pan in the oven to preheat for about 10 minutes. In a large bowl, combine the tomatoes and olive oil. Toss to coat. Add to the preheated pan and roast in the oven just until the tomatoes are tender and brown, about 20 minutes. Remove from the oven and drizzle with the vinegar. Add the garlic and toss gently. Divide among 4 plates. Top with the basil and shaved cheese. Season with the salt and pepper. Serve.

Balsamic-Glazed Cremini Mushroom Salad

These are John's famous mushrooms, which we use in many ways, from serving them as a salad to topping a grilled flatiron steak. Once you taste them, you will understand why they are famous. And they're quick to make. **Serves 4**

2 pounds **cremini mushrooms**

2 tablespoons extra-virgin **olive oil**

3 cloves **garlic**, minced

2 tablespoons **soy sauce**

2 tablespoons **sweet soy sauce**

2 tablespoons good-quality **balsamic vinegar**

Preheat the oven to 450°F on Convection Bake. Preheat an oven-proof sauté pan or skillet in the oven for 10 minutes. In a large bowl, combine the mushrooms and olive oil. Toss to coat. Add the mushrooms to the preheated pan and roast in the oven for about 15 minutes, or until they start to brown. In a small bowl, whisk together the garlic, soy sauce, sweet soy, and vinegar. Pour over the mushrooms and mix well. Roast another 2 minutes, or until well glazed. Remove from the oven and serve warm.

Roasted Potato Salad
with Crème Fraîche *and* Crab

This elegant salad would be **a lovely way to start a holiday meal** or any other special dinner. You can substitute a good-quality sour cream for the crème fraîche. **Serves 4**

2 pounds **Yukon Gold potatoes**, peeled and cut into 2-inch dice cubes

2 tablespoons extra-virgin **olive oil**

Salt and **cracked pepper** to taste

2 cloves **garlic**, minced

1 tablespoon minced fresh **chives**

1 large bunch **watercress**, stemmed

4 ounces fresh **crabmeat**, picked over for shell

½ cup **crème fraîche**

Preheat the oven to 425°F on Convection Bake. Place a roasting pan in the oven to preheat for 10 minutes. In a large bowl, combine the potatoes, olive oil, salt, and pepper. Toss to coat. Spread the potatoes on the preheated pan in a single layer. Roast in the oven until tender and golden brown, about 20 minutes. Remove from the oven and stir in the garlic.

Divide the potatoes among 4 plates. Sprinkle with the chives. Top with the watercress, then the crabmeat. Drizzle with the crème fraîche and serve.

Roasted Carrot Salad
with Pecans *and* Sherry Vinaigrette

Roasted sweet carrots and peppery watercress are a tasty combination. **The toasted pecans add a crispy finish** to this beautiful salad. The dressing also works well for a green salad. **Serves 4**

4 large **carrots**, peeled and cut into ½-inch dice

2 tablespoons extra-virgin **olive oil**

Salt and freshly ground **pepper** to taste

SHERRY VINAIGRETTE

2 tablespoons **sherry vinegar**

2 cloves **garlic**, minced

2 teaspoons **Dijon mustard**

6 tablespoons extra-virgin **olive oil**

Salt and freshly ground **pepper** to taste

2 bunches **watercress**, stemmed

½ cup **pecans**, toasted (see page 151) and chopped

Preheat the oven to 425°F on Convection Bake. Place a roasting pan in the oven to preheat for about 10 minutes. In a medium bowl, combine the carrots, olive oil, salt, and pepper. Toss to coat. Spread on the preheated pan in a single layer. Roast in the oven until tender and golden brown, about 20 minutes.

While the carrots are roasting, make the vinaigrette: In a small bowl, whisk the vinegar, garlic, and mustard together. Gradually whisk in the olive oil until incorporated. Season with the salt and pepper.

Divide the watercress among 4 salad plates. Top with the roasted carrots, drizzle with the vinaigrette, and sprinkle with the toasted pecans. Serve.

A SIDE DISH CAN SHOW OFF SEASONAL PRODUCE IN THE **BEST LIGHT** AND CAN TURN A SIMPLE ENTREE INTO A REALLY SPECIAL DINNER. MANY OF THE DISHES IN THIS CHAPTER ARE ROASTED, WHICH IS A GREAT WAY TO GET THE MOST OUT OF YOUR CONVECTION OVEN.

SIDE DISHES

Oven-Roasted Brussels Sprouts
with Orange Zest

Not everyone likes Brussels sprouts, but this recipe will win over even the biggest critics. **Using a hot oven and not over-cooking the sprouts helps to maximize their flavor.** **Serves 4**

1½ pounds **Brussels sprouts**, halved

2 tablespoons extra-virgin **olive oil**

Salt and freshly ground **pepper** to taste

2 cloves **garlic**, minced

Grated zest of 2 **oranges**

2 tablespoons good-quality **balsamic vinegar**

Preheat the oven to 425°F on Convection Bake. Place a roasting pan in the oven to preheat for about 10 minutes. In a large bowl, combine the sprouts, olive oil, salt, and pepper. Toss to coat. Spread on the preheated pan in one layer. Roast in the oven for about 6 minutes, or until crisp-tender. Transfer to a bowl and add the garlic, orange zest, and vinegar. Toss well and serve.

Roasted Fennel and Parsnips

Both the **fennel and parsnips benefit from roasting in a hot oven.** The fennel's anise flavor mellows, and the parsnips caramelize and sweeten nicely. **Serves 4**

2 large **fennel bulbs**, trimmed (reserve fronds), and cut into ½-inch dice

3 **parsnips**, peeled and cut into ½-inch dice

2 tablespoons extra-virgin **olive oil**

Salt and **cracked pepper** to taste

Preheat the oven to 425°F on Convection Bake. Place a roasting pan in the oven to preheat for about 10 minutes. In a medium bowl, combine the fennel, parsnips, olive oil, salt, and pepper. Toss well to coat. Spread the vegetables on the preheated pan in one layer. Roast in the oven until tender, about 20 minutes. Remove from the oven. Mince enough of the reserved fennel fronds to yield 1 tablespoon. Toss the vegetables with the minced fennel fronds and serve.

Oven-Roasted Green Beans

This may be a new way for you to cook green beans; it's fast, and **the beans intensify in flavor** in the process.

Serves 4

1 ½ pounds **green beans**, trimmed

1 tablespoon extra-virgin **olive oil**

Sea salt and freshly ground **pepper** to taste

Preheat the oven to 450°F on Convection Bake. Place a heavy baking sheet in the oven to preheat for about 10 minutes. In a large bowl, combine all the ingredients. Toss well to coat.

Spread the beans on the preheated baking sheet in one layer. Roast in the oven for about 4 minutes, or until crisp-tender. Serve.

Oven-Roasted Asparagus

This is about the only way we cook asparagus anymore—it's just so tasty and easy. **Serves 6**

1 ½ pounds **asparagus**, trimmed

1 tablespoon extra-virgin **olive oil**

Sea salt and freshly ground **pepper** to taste

Preheat the oven to 425°F on Convection Bake. Spread the asparagus on a baking sheet in one layer. Drizzle with the olive oil and season with salt and pepper. Roast in the oven for about 4 minutes, or until crisp-tender. Remove from the oven and serve.

Maple-Spice Butternut Squash Mash

This dish is a good substitute for the ever-present mashed potatoes, and the addition of maple syrup may entice your kids to eat squash. **Serves 4**

2 pounds **butternut squash**, halved and seeded

1 tablespoon extra-virgin **olive oil**

4 tablespoons unsalted **butter**

¼ cup **maple syrup**

½ cup **chicken stock**

½ teaspoon ground **cinnamon**

½ teaspoon ground **ginger**

Pinch of **cayenne pepper**

Salt to taste

Preheat the oven to 425°F on Convection Bake. Place the butternut squash in a roasting pan, cut side up. Drizzle with the olive oil. Roast in the oven until tender, about 40 minutes. Remove from the oven and scoop the flesh into a bowl.

In a small saucepan, combine the butter, syrup, stock, and spices. Bring to a boil over high heat. Add to the squash and mix well. Season with salt and serve.

Crispy Potato Rounds

These potatoes are like **crisp round oven fries.**
The paprika adds a smoky taste. **Serves 4**

4 unpeeled **Yukon Gold potatoes**, cut into ¼-inch-thick slices

2 tablespoons extra-virgin **olive oil**

Sea salt and freshly ground **pepper** to taste

½ teaspoon **sweet Spanish smoked paprika** (pimentón); optional

Preheat the oven to 425°F on Convection Bake. Place a sided baking sheet in the oven to preheat for about 10 minutes. In a medium bowl, combine all of the ingredients and toss well to coat. Spread the potatoes on the pan in one layer. Roast in the oven for 10 minutes, then turn the slices over and roast another 10 minutes, or until golden brown and cooked through. Remove from the oven and serve.

Parmesan-Herb Sweet Potato Fries

Our family loves these potatoes, especially with big juicy hamburgers. You can use Yukon Gold potatoes instead of sweet potatoes, if you like. **Serves 4**

3 large **sweet potatoes**, peeled and cut into wedges

1 tablespoon extra-virgin **olive oil**

Sea salt and freshly ground **pepper** to taste

¼ cup grated **Parmesan cheese**

½ teaspoon minced fresh **thyme**

¼ teaspoon minced fresh **rosemary**

Preheat the oven to 425°F on Convection Bake. Place a sided baking sheet in the oven to preheat for about 10 minutes. In a large bowl, combine the sweet potatoes, olive oil, salt, and pepper. Spread on the preheated pan in one layer. Bake in the oven for 10 minutes. Turn the potatoes over and bake 10 minutes longer, or until tender. In a small bowl, combine the cheese and herbs. Sprinkle over the potatoes and bake another 3 to 4 minutes, or until the cheese melts and browns. Remove from the oven and serve.

Basmati Pilaf

If you've never baked rice in the oven, you've missed the most foolproof way to cook perfect rice every time. **Serves 4**

1 tablespoon extra-virgin **olive oil**

2 cloves **garlic**, minced

½ **onion**, finely diced

1 cup **basmati rice**, rinsed and drained well

1½ cups **chicken** or **vegetable stock**

Salt and freshly ground **pepper** to taste

Preheat the oven to 350°F on Convection Bake. In a medium ovenproof saucepan, heat the olive oil over high heat. Add the garlic and onion and sauté until they start to brown, 3 to 4 minutes. Add the rice and toss well to coat it with the oil.

Add the stock and bring to a boil. Season with salt and pepper. Cover and bake in the oven for 15 minutes. Stir well. Re-cover and bake for another 15 minutes. Remove from the oven, fluff with a fork, and serve.

Spicy Coconut Basmati Rice

Either basmati or jasmine rice will fill your house with an amazing toasty smell. Omit the chilies if you think this might be too spicy for your family or guests. **Serves 4**

1 tablespoon **canola oil**

2 cloves **garlic**, minced

1 tablespoon minced fresh **ginger**

1 cup **basmati** or **jasmine rice**, rinsed and drained well

1 cup **chicken** or **vegetable stock**

3/4 cup **coconut milk**

2 **Thai bird chilies**, minced

Salt to taste

Preheat the oven to 350°F on Convection Bake. In a large ovenproof saucepan, heat the oil over high heat. Add the garlic and ginger and sauté for about 30 seconds. Add the rice to the pan and toss well to coat it with the oil. Add the stock, coconut milk, and chilies. Bring to a boil. Season with salt. Cover and bake in the oven for 15 minutes. Stir well. Re-cover and bake another 15 minutes. Remove from the oven, fluff with a fork, and serve.

HERE ARE SOME OF OUR FAMILY'S FAVORITE ENTREES,
FROM SAVANNAH'S CRISPY FOUR-CHEESE PASTA
TO OVEN-BAKED FISH AND CHIPS. **LIKE YOU, WE ARE BUSY,
SO MOST OF THE RECIPES ARE SIMPLE AND VERY DOABLE.**
WE ALSO INCLUDED A COUPLE OF FANCIER DISHES TO
SERVE FOR COMPANY OR SPECIAL OCCASIONS.

ENTREES

Perfect Roast Chicken

Everyone should know how to make the perfect roast chicken, so **we worked hard to make this recipe just right.** You can vary the seasonings depending on what you have on hand or what is in season. **Serves 4**

1 **lemon**

One 3½-pound **organic chicken**

2 teaspoons **kosher salt**

½ teaspoon freshly ground **pepper** to taste

1 head **garlic**, halved

2 **rosemary sprigs**

Preheat the oven to 450°F on Convection Bake. Grate the zest of the lemon and reserve the lemon. Season the chicken with the salt, pepper, and lemon zest. Cut the lemon in half and put it in the body cavity of the chicken along with the garlic and rosemary. Place a rack in a roasting pan and place the chicken on the rack. Roast the chicken in the oven for 45 to 50 minutes, or until an instant-read thermometer inserted in the thigh registers 155°F. Allow the chicken to rest for about 5 minutes, then carve and serve.

Thai Curry–Roasted Chicken Breasts

Thai curry paste adds spice to this glaze and an exotic flavor to everyday roasted chicken.

Serves 4

4 **chicken breast halves**

2 tablespoons **Thai green curry paste**

Grated zest and juice of 2 **limes**

1 tablespoon **brown sugar**

2 cloves **garlic**, minced

1 tablespoon grated fresh **ginger**

1 tablespoon **fish sauce** (optional)

Preheat the oven to 450°F on Convection Bake. Place a rack in a roasting pan and place the chicken breasts on the rack. Set aside.

In a small bowl, combine the curry paste, lime zest, lime juice, sugar, garlic, ginger, and fish sauce and mix well. Rub the curry mixture on top of the chicken. Roast the chicken in the oven for about 30 minutes, or until the juices run clear when the chicken is pierced with a knife. An instant-read thermometer inserted in the chicken should register 155°F. Remove from the oven and serve.

Easy Brined Chicken

Brining makes chicken juicier and more tender. The chicken must be brined overnight, so this is a good recipe for Sunday dinner. Serves 4

BRINE

4 cups good-quality
apple cider

3 cloves **garlic**, crushed

¼ cup **kosher salt**

12 **thyme sprigs**

One 3 ½-pound **organic
chicken**

1 tablespoon unsalted
butter, melted

½ teaspoon **cracked pepper**

To make the brine: In a medium bowl, combine the cider, garlic, salt, and thyme and whisk to dissolve the salt. Put the chicken in a large resealable plastic bag and pour the brine over the chicken. Seal and refrigerate overnight.

Preheat the oven to 450°F on Convection Bake. Remove the chicken from the brine and drain well. Place a rack in a roasting pan and place the chicken on the rack. Brush the chicken with melted butter and sprinkle with pepper. Roast in the oven for about 45 minutes, or until an instant-read thermometer inserted in the thigh registers 155°F. Remove from the oven and let rest for about 5 minutes. Carve and serve.

Braised Chicken Legs
with Cumin *and* Chilies

When chicken legs are braised they become very tender, and because they are dark meat they stay moist. The chilies and cumin add a bit of warmth to a comforting winter dish. **Serves 4**

4 **chicken legs** (with thighs)

Salt and freshly ground **pepper** to taste

½ cup **all-purpose flour**

1 tablespoon extra-virgin **olive oil**

1 small **onion**, diced

3 cloves **garlic**, minced

1 **ancho chili**, seeded and diced

3 **poblano chilies**, seeded and diced

3 cups **chicken stock**

2 tablespoons ground **cumin**

1 tablespoon unsalted **butter**

Preheat the oven to 375°F on Convection Bake. Season the chicken legs with salt and pepper and dredge in the flour. In a large ovenproof sauté pan or skillet, heat the oil over high heat. Add the chicken and brown well on both sides, about 4 minutes. Add the onion, garlic, and chilies to the pan and sauté for about 2 minutes. Add the stock and cumin and bring to a boil.

Cover and braise in the oven until tender, 35 to 40 minutes. Remove from the oven.

Transfer the chicken to a warmed platter. Place the roasting pan over high heat and skim the fat. Whisk in the butter and season to taste with salt and pepper. Pour the sauce over the chicken and serve.

Spicy Peanut Sauce Braised Chicken

This peanut sauce is one we have used for years at our restaurant. Made in a food processor, it is super simple. Also **try tossing it with noodles to serve as a side dish.** **Serves 4**

PEANUT SAUCE

1 teaspoon grated fresh **ginger**

1 teaspoon minced fresh **cilantro**

1 **jalapeno chili**, minced

¼ cup **red wine vinegar**

¼ cup **soy sauce**

½ cup **creamy peanut butter**

1 teaspoon **curry powder**

1 teaspoon **Asian sesame oil**

One 4-pound **organic chicken**, cut into serving pieces

Salt and freshly ground **pepper** to taste

1 tablespoon **canola oil**

2 cups **chicken broth**

Preheat the oven to 375°F on Convection Bake. To make the sauce: In a food processor, puree all of the sauce ingredients until smooth. Set aside.

Season the chicken with salt and pepper. In a large ovenproof sauté pan or skillet, heat the oil over high heat until smoking. Add the chicken, skin side down, and brown well on both sides, about 4 minutes. Add the stock, then whisk in the peanut sauce. Bring to a boil, cover, and braise in the oven until tender, 30 to 35 minutes. Remove from the oven and transfer the chicken to a warmed platter. Taste the sauce and adjust the seasoning. Pour over the chicken and serve.

Mahogany Roast Chicken

In this variation on roasted chicken, the glaze turns the chicken a beautiful golden brown. **The more you baste it, the more flavor the glaze adds.** You can also use the glaze on bone-in chicken breasts or even salmon fillets. **Serves 4**

MAHOGANY GLAZE

¼ cup **soy sauce**

1 tablespoon **Dijon mustard**

3 tablespoons **plum sauce**

2 cloves **garlic**, minced

1 tablespoon grated fresh **ginger**

1 teaspoon **chili sauce**

One 3 ½-pound **organic chicken**

Preheat the oven to 450°F on Convection Bake.

To make the glaze: In a small bowl, combine all the glaze ingredients and whisk until smooth.

Place a rack in a roasting pan and place the chicken on the rack. Brush the chicken liberally with the glaze and roast in the oven for about 45 minutes, brushing with the glaze every 15 minutes. The chicken is done when an instant-read thermometer inserted in the thigh registers 155°F. Remove from the oven and let rest for about 5 minutes. Carve the chicken and serve.

Paella

The ultimate one-pot meal: chicken, seafood, and rice cooked in a flavorful broth. John and I worked hard to keep this recipe simple, so don't be discouraged by its length; **it just has lots of yummy ingredients.** Panfry the leftovers the next day for a wonderful lunch.

Serves 6

2 tablespoons extra-virgin **olive oil**

1½ pounds **boneless, skinless chicken thighs**

Salt and freshly ground **pepper** to taste

1 small **onion**, diced

4 cloves **garlic**, minced

1 **red bell pepper**, seeded, deribbed, and sliced

1 tablespoon **sweet Spanish smoked paprika** (pimentón); optional

1 tablespoon **dried oregano**

Pinch of **red pepper flakes**

2 cups **Arborio rice**

2½ cups **chicken stock**

1 teaspoon **saffron threads**

1 cup good-quality canned **tomatoes**, chopped

1 pound **clams**, scrubbed

16 large **shrimp** (21 to 30 per pound) in the shell, deveined

1 **lemon**, cut into wedges

Preheat the oven to 400°F on Convection Bake. In a 12-inch oven-proof sauté pan or skillet, heat the oil until smoking. Season the chicken thighs with salt and pepper. Add to the pan and brown well on both sides, about 4 minutes. Add the onion, garlic, bell pepper, paprika, oregano, and pepper flakes and sauté for 4 minutes. Add the rice and stir to coat well in the olive oil. Add 2 cups of the stock, the saffron, and tomatoes and bring to a boil. Add salt and pepper to taste. Cover and bake in the oven for 10 minutes.

Remove from the oven, stir gently, and add the clams, shrimp, and remaining ½ cup stock. Cover and bake for 20 minutes, or until the clams have opened and the shrimp are pink. Remove from the oven. Discard any clams that have not opened. Serve at once, with the lemon wedges.

Perfect Sunday Roast
with Pan Gravy

We love making a roast on a lazy Sunday. **It's a one-pan wonder,** and that makes us happy. Comforting and soul satisfying, this dish makes a great ending to a weekend with family and friends. **Serves 4**

One **3-pound beef eye of round roast**

Salt and freshly ground **pepper** to taste

1 tablespoon extra-virgin **olive oil**

2 **carrots**, peeled and cut into medium dice

8 **Yukon Gold potatoes**, peeled and halved

1 tablespoon minced fresh **thyme**

3 cloves **garlic**, crushed

1 tablespoon **all-purpose flour**

½ cup **dry red wine**

1 cup **chicken stock**

1 tablespoon **Dijon mustard**

¼ cup **heavy cream**

Preheat the oven to 375°F on Convection Bake. Season the beef with salt and pepper. In a large roasting pan, heat the oil over high heat until smoking. Add the roast and brown on all sides, about 4 minutes. Remove the meat from pan and add the carrots, potatoes, thyme, and garlic. Place the meat on top of the vegetables and roast for about 40 minutes, or until an instant-read thermometer inserted in the center of the roast registers 130°F.

Transfer the roast to a plate, tent loosely with aluminum foil, and set aside to rest. If the vegetable are not cooked through, continue roasting them until tender. Remove the vegetables from the roasting pan and place the pan over medium heat. Add the flour to the pan and whisk. Add the wine and cook to reduce by half. Add the stock, mustard, and cream and cook, whisking occasionally, until thickened, about 3 minutes. Slice the meat and place on a warmed platter with the vegetables. Serve the gravy alongside.

Provençal Pork Loin Roast

We love preparing pork loin this way; **we even take it camping with us.** If the pork starts to brown too fast, tent it with aluminum foil. Oranges and even grapefruit work well in this recipe. **Serves 4**

One 2 ½- to 3-pound **boneless pork loin roast**

3 cloves **garlic**, minced

¼ cup **honey**

1 tablespoon **herbes de Provence**

1 **lemon**, scrubbed and thinly sliced

Salt and freshly ground **pepper** to taste

1 tablespoon extra-virgin **olive oil**

Cut 3 diagonal slices in the fat of the pork, about ¼ inch deep. Lay a large piece of plastic wrap on a work surface and place the pork loin, fat side up, on top of the plastic wrap. In a small bowl, combine the garlic, honey, and herbs and mix well. Pour over the pork loin. Overlap the lemon slices to cover the top of the roast and wrap it tightly in plastic wrap. Refrigerate for at least 2 hours or up to 24 hours.

Preheat the oven to 450°F on Convection Bake. Remove the plastic wrap and lemon slices from the pork. Season the pork well with salt and pepper and place, fat side down, in a roasting pan. Drizzle with olive oil and roast in the oven for about 30 minutes, or until an instant-read thermometer inserted in the center of the roast registers 140°F. Remove from the oven and let rest for about 5 minutes. Slice and serve.

3 **onions**, cut into ½-inch dice

1 tablespoon **sea salt**

1 teaspoon **cracked pepper** to taste

2 teaspoons minced fresh **sage**

2 teaspoons minced fresh **rosemary**

3 cloves **garlic**, minced

Pinch of **red pepper flakes**

1 **crown roast of pork** (about 7 pounds)

1 tablespoon extra-virgin **olive oil**

Wild Rice Stuffing (recipe follows)

Crown Roast of Pork
with Wild Rice Stuffing

When you bring a crown roast of pork to the table, you will be greeted with plenty of oohs and ahhs, and **no one needs to know just how easy it was to cook.** Fill the crown roast with the separately baked stuffing just before serving so the roast will cook evenly. **Serves 10**

Preheat the oven to 350°F on Convection Bake. Spread the onions in a roasting pan and set aside.

In a small bowl, combine the salt, pepper, sage, rosemary, garlic, and pepper flakes. Mix well. Place the pork on top of the onions. Coat the pork with the olive oil and rub the salt mixture on the inside and outside of the meat. Roast in the oven for about 2 hours, or until an instant-read thermometer inserted in the center of the meat registers 140°F. Remove from the oven and let rest for about 5 minutes. Fill with the stuffing and serve warm, with the roasted onions. Cut into chops at the table.

2 tablespoons unsalted **butter**

1 large **onion**, diced

3 cloves **garlic**, minced

1 ½ cups **port wine**

4 cups diced **day-old bread**

2 cups cooked **wild rice**

3 **eggs**, lightly beaten

1 cup **chicken** or **turkey stock**

½ teaspoon minced fresh **rosemary**

1 teaspoon minced fresh **sage**

1 teaspoon minced fresh **thyme**

½ cup **hazelnuts**, toasted, skinned (see page 151), and coarsely chopped

Salt and freshly ground **pepper** to taste

Wild Rice Stuffing   **Serves 6**

Preheat the oven to 375°F on Convection Bake. Grease a 6-cup baking dish.

In a large sauté pan or skillet, melt the butter over high heat and sauté the onion until tender, about 3 minutes. Add the garlic and sauté for 1 minute. Add the wine and cook until the wine is almost evaporated, about 4 minutes. Transfer the mixture to a large bowl and let cool.

Add the bread and wild rice to the cooled onion mixture and mix well.

Add the eggs and mix well. Add enough of the stock to moisten the bread well. Stir in the herbs, hazelnuts, and salt and pepper. Make a small patty and cook in a little oil in a small sauté pan or skillet until cooked through, about 4 minutes. Taste, then adjust the seasoning of the uncooked stuffing if necessary.

Spread the stuffing in the prepared baking dish. Cover with aluminum foil and bake in the oven for 50 minutes. Remove from the oven, uncover, and serve hot.

Slow-Roasted Pork Loin Roast
with Herbs *and* Garlic

When you have extra time, slow roasting can make a big difference in the texture and flavor of meat. **This technique yields a tender, juicy roast**, especially when the meat is not boned. **Serves 4**

3 pounds **bone-in pork loin roast**

1 clove **garlic**, thinly sliced

1 teaspoon minced fresh **rosemary**

½ teaspoon minced fresh **oregano**

1 teaspoon minced fresh **basil**

Grated zest of 1 **lemon**

Salt and freshly ground **pepper** to taste

2 teaspoons extra-virgin **olive oil**

Preheat the oven to 275°F on Convection Bake. Using a sharp knife, make a cut in the roast following the bone but not cutting completely through the meat to the other end. In the opening, spread the garlic, herbs, and lemon zest. Sprinkle with salt and pepper. Using kitchen twine, tie the roast together at ½-inch intervals. Coat with the olive oil and sprinkle with salt and pepper.

Put the meat in a roasting pan, fat side up, and roast in the oven for about 1 hour and 10 minutes, or until an instant-read thermometer inserted in the center of the meat and not touching bone registers 140°F. Remove from the oven and let rest for about 5 minutes. Remove the meat from the bones, slice, and serve.

Pork Medallions
Stuffed *with* Apple *and* Blue Cheese

Pears work well for this recipe also, and if you don't care for blue cheese **try a good melting cheese such as fontina or Gouda.** Make sure you open the pocket of the meat so you can fit more stuffing in the medallions. **Serves 4**

2 tablespoons
extra-virgin **olive oil**

¼ cup diced **onion**

2 cloves **garlic**, minced

1 **Granny Smith apple**,
peeled, cored, and diced

1 teaspoon minced
fresh **thyme**

¼ cup good-quality
blue cheese

Salt and freshly ground
pepper to taste

4 boneless
center cut **pork chops**

Preheat the oven to 425°F on Convection Bake. In a large sauté pan or skillet, heat 1 tablespoon of the oil over high heat. Add the onion and sauté for 2 minutes. Add the garlic and sauté for 1 minute. Add the apple and thyme and sauté until the apple is tender, about 3 minutes. Remove from the pan and let cool. Stir in the blue cheese, salt, and pepper. Place in a pastry bag without a tip and set aside while you prepare the pork.

Make a cut about 1 inch long and 1½ inches deep in the side of each chop.

Using your finger, pull the meat apart slightly to enlarge the pocket. Fill each pocket with about one-fourth of the stuffing. In a large ovenproof sauté pan or skillet, heat the remaining 1 tablespoon oil over high heat until smoking. Season the pork with salt and pepper on both sides and place in the pan. Brown well on both sides, about 4 minutes. Place the pan in the oven and bake for 7 minutes, or until an instant-read thermometer inserted into a chop registers 140°F. Remove from the oven and serve.

Braised Short Ribs
with Tomatillos *and* Chilies

Tomatillos are a wonderful ingredient in this dish, as they add an acidic tang that balances the richness of the short ribs. We like to serve this over rice so the rice soaks up the braising liquid. **Serves 4**

1 tablespoon ground **cumin**

1 tablespoon **mild chili powder**

1 tablespoon **sweet Spanish smoked paprika** (pimentón); optional

Salt and freshly ground **pepper** to taste

4 pounds **beef short ribs**

2 tablespoons extra-virgin **olive oil**

1 **onion**, diced

3 cloves **garlic**, minced

1 pound **tomatillos**, husked, rinsed, and quartered

3 **Anaheim chilies**, seeded and diced

4 cups **chicken stock**

Grated zest and juice of 1 **orange**

2 cups cooked **basmati rice** (optional)

Preheat the oven to 425°F on Convection Bake. In a small bowl, combine the cumin, chili powder, paprika, salt, and pepper. Season the ribs with the spice mixture.

In a large ovenproof sauté pan or skillet, heat the oil over high heat until hot. Add the short ribs and brown well on all sides, about 5 minutes. Add the onion and garlic and sauté for 3 minutes. Add the tomatillos, chilies, stock, orange zest, and juice and bring to a boil. Cover and braise in the oven until very tender, about 1 1/2 hours. Remove from the oven and skim the fat from the sauce. Season with salt and pepper to taste. Serve with the sauce and rice, if desired.

New York Steaks
with Fontina-Hazelnut Bread Crumbs

John and I had a steak prepared like this in the great food city of Chicago and wanted to re-create it at home. We loved the toasty bread crumbs with bits of cheese on top of the succulent steak. **Serves 4**

1 cup (4 ounces) shredded **fontina cheese**

½ cup **hazelnuts**, toasted, skinned (see page 151), and ground

1 cup fresh **bread crumbs**, toasted (see page 151)

1 teaspoons **Dijon mustard**

1 clove **garlic**, minced

2 tablespoons extra-virgin **olive oil**

Four 10-ounce **New York steaks**

Salt and freshly ground **pepper** to taste

Preheat the oven on high on Convection Broil. In a medium bowl, combine the cheese, hazelnuts, bread crumbs, mustard, garlic, and 1 tablespoon olive oil. Mix well. Set aside.

Place the steaks on a broiler pan and coat on both sides with the remaining 1 tablespoon oil. Season well with salt and pepper. Place under the broiler about 4 inches from the heat source and cook for 4 minutes. Turn the steaks over and cook for 2 minutes for medium-rare. Remove from the oven and top each steak with one-fourth of the bread crumb mixture. Replace under the broiler for 1 minute, or until golden brown. Remove from the oven and serve.

Chuck Roast
with Dried Cranberries *and* Sage

In our mind, there is nothing better than taking an inexpensive cut of meat and turning it into something special. Cooked just until tender and flavored with tangy cranberries and savory sage, this chuck roast is modern and yummy. **Serves 4**

1 tablespoon extra-virgin **olive oil**

One 3-pound **beef chuck roast**

Salt and freshly ground **pepper** to taste

1 **onion**, diced

3 cloves **garlic**, minced

1 tablespoon minced fresh **sage**

1 cup **dried cranberries**

1 cup **dry red wine**

¼ cup **balsamic vinegar**

4 cups **chicken stock**

Preheat the oven to 425°F on Convection Bake. In a large ovenproof sauté pan or skillet, heat the oil over high until smoking. Season the roast with salt and pepper. Put the roast in the pan and brown on all sides, about 5 minutes. Add the onion, garlic, and sage and sauté until tender, about 4 minutes. Add the cranberries, red wine, and vinegar and cook to reduce by half. Add the stock and bring to a boil.

Cover and roast in the oven for 1 hour, or until very tender. Remove from the oven and transfer the roast to a cutting board. Slice the roast and place on a warmed platter. Skim the fat from the sauce. Taste and adjust the seasoning. Ladle the sauce over the roast and serve.

John's Parmesan Meat Loaf

This great meat loaf is even better the next day in meat loaf sandwiches. You can also form the mixture into meatballs and bake them for about 20 minutes in a roasting pan. **Serves 4**

1 pound **ground beef**

1 pound bulk **mild Italian sausage**

1 tablespoon extra-virgin **olive oil**

1 **onion**, finely diced

4 cloves **garlic**

3/4 cup grated **Parmesan cheese**

2 **eggs**, lightly beaten

3/4 cup **bread crumbs**, toasted (see page 151)

3 tablespoons **tomato paste**

2 tablespoons **Dijon mustard**

1 tablespoon **Worcestershire sauce**

1 tablespoon **Tabasco sauce**

Salt and **cracked pepper** to taste

Preheat the oven to 375°F on Convection Bake. In a large bowl, combine the beef and sausage. Mix well and set aside. In a small sauté pan or skillet, heat the oil over high heat and sauté the onion and garlic until tender, about 4 minutes. Remove from the pan and let cool. Stir into the meat mixture. Add the cheese, eggs, and bread crumbs and mix well. Add the tomato paste, mustard, Worcestershire sauce, Tabasco, salt, and pepper. Mix well.

Make a very small patty of the meat loaf mixture and cook in a sauté pan. Taste, then adjust the seasoning of the meat loaf mixture if necessary. Press the mixture into a 6-cup loaf pan and bake in the oven for 45 minutes. Remove from the oven and drain off the fat. Carefully unmold, slice, and serve.

Curried Rack of Lamb
with Yogurt Sauce

Rack of lamb is definitely a special-occasion dish. **This recipe is great for a company dinner,** because you can brown the lamb ahead of time and finish it in the oven just before serving. The yogurt sauce can also be made ahead. **Serves 4**

2 tablespoons extra-virgin **olive oil**

1 **rack of lamb**, trimmed and Frenched

Salt and freshly ground **pepper** to taste

1 tablespoon **curry powder**

2 cloves **garlic**, minced

1 tablespoon grated fresh **ginger**

2 teaspoons **soy sauce**

YOGURT SAUCE

¾ cup **Greek yogurt**

2 cloves **garlic**, minced

½ teaspoon minced fresh **mint**

1 teaspoon minced fresh **cilantro**

Salt and freshly ground **pepper** to taste

Preheat the oven to 400°F on Convection Bake. In a large ovenproof sauté pan or skillet, heat 1 tablespoon of the oil over high heat until smoking. Season the lamb with salt and pepper. Place the lamb, meat side down, in the pan and brown well on both sides, about 4 minutes. Remove from the heat.

In a small bowl, combine the curry powder, garlic, ginger, the remaining 1 tablespoon olive oil, and soy sauce and mix well. Spread the curry mixture on the meat sides of the lamb. Roast in the oven for 15 minutes, or until an instant-read thermometer inserted in the center of the meat registers 130°F.

While the lamb is cooking, make the yogurt sauce: In a small bowl, combine all the ingredients and mix well. Refrigerate until ready to use, or for up to 2 weeks.

Remove the lamb from the oven and let rest for 3 minutes. Slice and serve with the yogurt sauce.

Braised Lamb
with Cilantro, Mint, *and* Coconut Milk

We taught this recipe in our cooking class one winter, and our students raved about it. This dish cries out for mashed potatoes or steamed rice to soak up every bit of the braising liquid. **Serves 4**

3 pounds **boneless leg of lamb**, cut into 1-inch cubes

Salt and freshly ground **pepper** to taste

1 tablespoon **canola oil**

1 tablespoon minced fresh **ginger**

3 cloves **garlic**, minced

2 teaspoons minced fresh **cilantro**

2 teaspoons minced fresh **mint**

2 cups **chicken** or **lamb stock**

2 cups **coconut milk**

Grated zest and juice of 2 **limes**

Preheat the oven to 375°F on Convection Bake. Season the lamb with salt and pepper. In a large oven-proof sauté pan or skillet, heat the oil over high heat until smoking. Add the lamb and sear until brown on all sides, 4 to 5 minutes. Add the ginger and garlic and sauté until fragrant. Add the cilantro, mint, stock, coconut milk, lime zest, and juice. Bring to a boil. Cover and braise in the oven until tender, about 45 minutes. Remove from the oven and skim the fat from the sauce. Season with salt and pepper to taste. Serve.

Broiled Lamb Chops
with Salsa Verde

The salsa verde can be made days ahead, and the lamb cooks in less than 10 minutes, making this the star of a quick and tasty dinner. **Serves 4**

SALSA VERDE

1 bunch **basil**

1 bunch **flat-leaf parsley**

1 bunch **mint leaves**

4 cloves **garlic**, minced

Grated zest and juice of
2 **lemons**

2 tablespoons **capers**

1 **anchovy**

⅓ cup extra-virgin **olive oil**

Salt and freshly ground
pepper to taste

Eight 4-ounce **lamb chops**

1 tablespoon extra-virgin
olive oil

Salt and freshly ground
pepper to taste

Preheat the oven on high on Convection Broil, with the broiler pan on the top rack.

To make the salsa: In a food processor, combine the basil, parsley, mint, garlic, lemon zest, juice, capers, and anchovy. Process until chopped. With the machine running, slowly add the olive oil. Season with salt and pepper. Set aside.

Coat the lamb chops with olive oil and season with salt and pepper. Place the chops on the hot broiler pan and cook for 4 minutes on each side for medium-rare, or until an instant-read thermometer inserted in the meat registers 130°F. Remove from the oven and serve, topped with salsa verde.

Broiled Prawns
with Tangy Tartar Sauce

Homemade tartar sauce is easy to make and tastier than bottled sauce. You can also use the sauce on Crispy Oven-Baked Fish and Chips (page 91). **Serves 4**

TANGY TARTAR SAUCE

1 **egg yolk**

Grated zest and juice of 1 **lemon**

2 cloves **garlic**, minced

2 teaspoons **Dijon mustard**

1 cup extra-virgin **olive oil**

1 tablespoon minced
fresh **tarragon**

2 teaspoons **capers**, minced

1 tablespoon minced **gherkins**

2 teaspoons **cayenne sauce**

Salt and freshly ground
pepper to taste

24 extra-large **shrimp** (16 to 20
per pound), shelled and deveined

2 tablespoons extra-virgin **olive oil**

Salt and freshly ground
pepper to taste

Soak 4 wooden skewers in water for 30 minutes.

Preheat the oven on high on Convection Broil. To make the tartar sauce: In a food processor, combine the egg yolk, lemon zest, juice, garlic, and mustard. Process until smooth. With the machine running, gradually add the olive oil in a thin stream until the sauce is thick and smooth. Pour into a bowl and stir in the tarragon, capers, gherkins, and cayenne sauce. Season with salt and pepper. Cover and refrigerate until ready to use, or for up to 1 week.

Thread 6 shrimp on each skewer, going through the head and tail of each shrimp. Coat with the olive oil and sprinkle with salt and pepper. Place on a broiler pan and place under the broiler about 4 inches from the heat source. Cook for 2 minutes on each side, or until pink. Serve with the tartar sauce on the side.

Oven-Poached Halibut
with Pinot Gris Broth

Oven poaching keeps fish moist, and also yields a flavorful broth. Any white-fleshed fish in season can be substituted for the halibut. **Serves 4**

1 bottle (750ml)
Pinot Gris wine

3 cloves **garlic**, minced

2 tablespoons minced
fresh **tarragon**

Four 6-ounce **halibut fillets**

2 tablespoons unsalted **butter**

Salt and freshly ground
pepper to taste

Preheat the oven to 375°F on Convection Bake. In a large ovenproof nonreactive sauté pan or skillet, bring the wine to a boil over high heat. Add the garlic and tarragon and cook for 4 to 5 minutes. Add the halibut and poach in the oven for about 10 minutes, or until opaque throughout. Remove the pan from the oven. Using a slotted metal spatula, carefully transfer the halibut to a platter and cover to keep warm. Place the pan over high heat and bring to a boil. Whisk in the butter and season with salt and pepper. Pour the hot broth over the fish and serve.

Crispy Oven-Baked Fish and Chips

Fish and chips are a family favorite, but deep-frying is messy and not exactly healthy. **We created a healthier option** with this oven-baked recipe. Serve with Tangy Tartar Sauce if desired (see page 86). **Serves 4**

CHIPS

5 unpeeled **Yukon Gold potatoes**, cut into wedges

2 tablespoons extra-virgin **olive oil**

Sea salt and **cracked pepper** to taste

Flour for dredging

3 **eggs**, lightly beaten

4 cups fresh **bread crumbs**, toasted (see page 151)

1 cup grated **Parmesan cheese**

1 tablespoon **dried basil**

Pinch of **cayenne pepper**

1 tablespoon extra-virgin **olive oil**

2 pounds **halibut** or **cod**, cut into 2-inch pieces

Salt and freshly ground **pepper** to taste

2 **lemons**, cut into wedges

Preheat the oven to 425°F on Convection Bake. To make the chips: Place a rimmed baking sheet in the oven to heat for about 10 minutes. In a medium bowl, combine the potatoes, olive oil, salt, and pepper. Set aside.

Place the flour on a plate and put the beaten eggs in a bowl. In another shallow bowl, combine the bread crumbs, cheese, basil, and cayenne and mix well. Drizzle a roasting pan with the olive oil. Season the fish with salt and pepper. Dredge the fish in the flour, then in the eggs, and then in the bread crumbs. Place in the roasting pan and set aside.

Add the potatoes to the preheated baking sheet and bake in the oven for 10 minutes. After the potatoes have cooked for 10 minutes, place the fish in the oven and cook both the potatoes and the fish for about 10 minutes more, or until the until the fish is golden brown. Remove the potatoes and fish from the oven and serve with the lemon wedges.

Oven-Roasted Salmon
with Mustard-Orange Glaze

The Chinese mustard in this recipe gives the glaze a bit of a kick; you can cut the amount of mustard in half for a milder taste. Use this glaze on other flavorful fish, such as tuna. **Serves 4**

Four 6-ounce **salmon fillets**

Salt and freshly ground **pepper** to taste

1 tablespoon **canola oil**

MUSTARD GLAZE

2 teaspoons **dry Chinese mustard** or **dry English mustard**

2 teaspoons **warm water**

1 tablespoon **soy sauce**

1 tablespoon grated fresh **ginger**

2 tablespoons **honey**

1 tablespoon **frozen orange juice concentrate**

Preheat the oven to 375°F on Convection Bake. Season the salmon with salt and pepper. Drizzle a roasting pan with the oil and place the salmon in the pan.

To make the glaze: In a small bowl, combine all the ingredients and mix well. Brush the fillets thickly with the glaze and bake in the oven for about 10 minutes, or until still slightly translucent in the center. Remove from the oven and serve.

Pizza *with* Arugula *and* Blue Cheese

Convection ovens are great for cooking pizza because **the setting gives you a crispy brown crust in just a few minutes.** **Makes two 12-inch pizzas; serves 4**

Pizza Dough (page 148)

2 tablespoons
extra-virgin **olive oil**

3 cloves **garlic**, minced

½ teaspoon **red pepper flakes**

½ teaspoon **sea salt**

1 cup (5 ounces) crumbled
good-quality **blue cheese**

1 bunch **arugula**

Preheat the oven to 500°F on Convection Bake, with a baking stone inside if you have one.

Divide the dough in half. On a well-floured board, roll or stretch one half of the dough to a 12-inch round. If not using a baking stone, place the round on a greased pizza pan. Otherwise, dust a pizza peel with flour and place the dough on the peel.

In a small bowl, combine the olive oil, garlic, pepper flakes, and salt. Mix well. Spread the olive oil mixture on the pizza (reserving half of the mixture) and sprinkle with half of the blue cheese. Slide the pizza onto the hot stone or place the pizza pan in the oven and bake until the edges of the dough are golden brown, about 5 minutes. Remove from the oven and top with half of the arugula. Let cool for about 2 minutes. Slice and serve. Repeat for the second pizza.

Pizza *with* Three Cheeses, Tomatoes, *and* Olives

This is our most traditional-style pizza recipe, even though it doesn't have tomato sauce. You can always add tomato sauce, homemade or good-quality commercial sauce, if you like. **This recipe is a kid favorite.**

Makes two 12-inch pizzas; serves 4

Pizza Dough (page 148)

2 tablespoons extra-virgin **olive oil**

2 cloves **garlic**, minced

½ teaspoon **sea salt**

4 **plum** (Roma) **tomatoes**, thinly sliced

½ cup (2 ounces) grated **Parmesan cheese**

½ cup (2 ounces) shredded **fontina cheese**

½ cup (2 ounces) shredded **mozzarella cheese**

½ cup chopped **cured black olives**, such as kalamata

Preheat the oven to 500°F on Convection Bake, with a baking stone inside, if you have one.

Divide the dough in half. On a well-floured board, roll or stretch one half of the dough to a 12-inch round. If not using a baking stone, place the round on a greased pizza pan. Otherwise, dust a pizza peel with flour and place the dough on the peel. In a small bowl, mix the olive oil, garlic, and salt together. Brush the dough with the olive oil mixture (reserving half of the mixture). Place half of the sliced tomatoes on the dough and top with half of each cheese and half of the olives.

Slide the pizza onto the preheated stone or place the pizza pan in the oven and bake until the edges of the dough are golden brown, about 5 minutes. Remove from the oven and let rest for 3 minutes. Slice and serve. Repeat for the second pizza.

Pizza *with* Fried Shallots, Speck, *and* Gouda Cheese

Speck is a smoked cured meat from northern Italy. If not available, use prosciutto. **Frying the shallots gives them a sweet, crispy texture.** **Makes two 12-inch pizzas; serves 4**

6 **shallots**, thinly sliced

½ cup **all-purpose flour**

¼ cup extra-virgin **olive oil**

2 cloves **garlic**, minced

½ teaspoon **sea salt**

Pizza Dough (page 148)

4 ounces thinly sliced **speck** or **prosciutto**, cut into julienne

1 cup (4 ounces) shredded **Gouda cheese**

2 tablespoons julienned fresh **basil**

Preheat the oven to 500°F on Convection Bake, with a baking stone inside, if you have one.

In a small bowl, combine the shallots and flour. Dredge the sliced shallots in the flour, then shake the excess flour from the shallots, using a sieve. In a small sauté pan or skillet, heat the oil over high heat until shimmering. Add the shallots and cook until golden brown, about 2 minutes. Using a slotted spoon, transfer to paper towels to drain. Remove the pan from the heat and add the garlic and salt. Set aside.

Divide the dough in half. On a well-floured board, roll or stretch one half of the dough to a 12-inch round. If not using a baking stone, place the round on a greased pizza pan. Otherwise, dust a pizza peel with flour and place the dough on the peel. Brush the dough with about half of the olive oil mixture. Sprinkle the dough with half of the fried shallots, half of the julienned speck or prosciutto, half of the Gouda, and half of the basil.

Slide the pizza onto the hot stone or place the pizza pan in the oven and bake until the edges of the dough are golden brown, about 5 minutes. Remove from the oven and let rest for 3 minutes. Slice and serve. Repeat for the second pizza.

Pizza *with* Mushrooms *and* Fontina

This pizza uses a nontraditional cream sauce, like that of a pizza we had in France. Wait till you try it—it's rich, but so good. We sometimes use caramelized onions on this pizza instead of sliced mushrooms. **Makes: two 12-inch pizzas; serves 4**

CREAM SAUCE

1 cup **dry white wine**

2 cloves **garlic**, minced

1 ½ cups **heavy cream**

Salt and freshly ground **pepper** to taste

Pizza Dough (page 148)

1 cup (4 ounces) shredded **fontina cheese**

3 ounces **button mushrooms**, thinly sliced

To make the sauce: In a small saucepan, combine the wine and garlic. Bring to a boil over medium heat and cook to reduce by half, about 5 minutes. Stir in the cream and cook until the sauce is thickened and coats the back of the spoon, 5 to 6 minutes. Season with salt and pepper. Remove from the heat and let cool.

Preheat the oven to 500°F on Convection Bake, with a baking stone inside, if you have one.

Divide the dough in half. On a well-floured board, roll or stretch one half of the dough to a 12-inch round. If not using a baking stone, place the round on a greased pizza pan. Otherwise, dust a pizza peel with flour and place the dough on the peel. Gently spread half of the sauce on the pizza, then sprinkle with half of the cheese and mushrooms. Slide the pizza onto the hot stone or place the pizza pan in the oven and bake until the edges of the dough are golden brown, about 5 minutes. Remove from the oven and let cool for 2 minutes, then slice and serve. Repeat for the second pizza.

Black Bean and Fried Corn Enchiladas

John cooks corn this way all summer. In enchiladas, **it adds a crisp texture and a touch of sweet flavor.** Enchiladas freeze well, so I often make two pans and freeze one for a later dinner. **Serves 4**

2 tablespoons unsalted **butter**

2 cups **corn kernels** (about 4 ears of corn)

Salt and freshly ground **pepper** to taste

3 cups cooked **black beans**

2 cups (10 ounces) crumbled **queso fresco** or **mild feta cheese**

2 cups (8 ounces) shredded **sharp Cheddar cheese**

1 tablespoon ground **cumin**

2 teaspoons **mild chili powder**

1 teaspoon **sweet Spanish smoked paprika** (pimentón); optional

3½ cups **mild enchilada sauce**

12 **corn tortillas**

Preheat the oven to 375°F on Convection Bake. In a large sauté pan or skillet, melt the butter over high heat until bubbling. Add the corn and sauté until the corn starts to brown, about 5 minutes. Season with salt and pepper. Pour into a large bowl. Add the black beans, 1 cup of the queso fresco or feta, and all of the Cheddar cheese. Mix well and set aside.

Heat a large sauté pan or skillet over high heat until very hot and add the cumin, chili powder, and paprika, if using; toast until fragrant, about 30 seconds. Add the sauce to the pan and cook for 3 to 4 minutes. Season with salt and pepper to taste. Set aside.

Heat a medium nonstick sauté pan or skillet over medium heat. Place 1 tortilla in the pan and cook to warm briefly, 1 minute. Remove from the pan and place about ¼ cup of the filling in a line down the center of the warm tortilla. Roll the tortilla and place, seam side down, in the prepared dish. Repeat with the remaining tortillas. Pour the sauce over the tortillas and top with the remaining queso fresco or feta. Bake in the oven until golden brown and bubbling, about 25 minutes. Remove from the oven and serve.

Eggplant Steaks
with Tomato-Olive Compote

Eggplant is a great vehicle, as it will absorb any flavors that are paired with it. The marinade mellows any bitterness of the eggplant, and broiling gives it a wonderful caramelized texture. **Serves 4**

3 cloves minced **garlic**

¼ cup **balsamic vinegar**

⅓ cup extra-virgin **olive oil**, plus 1 tablespoon

Salt and freshly ground **pepper** to taste

2 unpeeled large **eggplants**, cut into eight 1-inch-thick crosswise slices

3 ripe **tomatoes**, seeded and finely chopped

1 cup **kalamata olives**, pitted and finely chopped

2 tablespoons minced fresh **basil**

¾ cup (3 ounces) grated **Parmesan cheese**

¾ cup fresh **bread crumbs**, toasted (see page 151)

Preheat the oven on high on Convection Broil. In a large bowl, combine the garlic, balsamic vinegar, and the ⅓ cup olive oil. Whisk until smooth. Season with salt and pepper. Add the eggplant slices and toss well. Set aside. In a medium bowl, combine the tomatoes, olives, basil, and the 1 tablespoon olive oil. Season with salt and pepper to taste; set aside. In a small bowl, mix the Parmesan cheese and bread crumbs together. Set aside.

Place the eggplant on a broiler pan in a single layer and place under the broiler 4 inches from the heat source. Broil for 4 minutes on each side. Remove from the broiler and spread the tomato mixture evenly on all 8 slices. Top with the bread crumb mixture. Place under the broiler again for about 1 minute, or until golden brown and crispy. Serve at once.

Potato-Artichoke Pie

This pie is a good choice for a spring evening when the weather is still a bit unpredictable, as **it can be served either warm or at room temperature.** We use fontina cheese because it adds a creamy texture, but any good shredding cheese, such as Monterey Jack, will work in this recipe. **Serves 4**

Cappy's Pie Dough (page 149)

1 tablespoon extra-virgin **olive oil**

1 large **onion**, diced

3 cloves **garlic**, sliced

2 cups **artichoke hearts**, coarsely chopped

4 large **Yukon Gold potatoes**, cooked, peeled, and diced

1 ½ cups (6 ounces) shredded **fontina cheese**

1 tablespoons minced fresh **basil**

Salt and freshly ground **pepper** to taste

1 ½ cups fresh **bread crumbs**, toasted (see page 151)

Preheat the oven to 400°F on Convection Bake. On a well-floured board, roll the dough out to an 11-inch round. Fold and place in a 9-inch pie plate. Trim the overhang to 1 inch. Turn the overhang under and flute the edges. Bake in the oven until the dough is set, about 10 minutes. Remove from the oven and set aside.

In a large sauté pan or skillet, heat the oil over high heat until smoking. Add the onion and sauté until it starts to brown, about 5 minutes. Add the garlic and cook until it starts to brown, about 2 minutes. Transfer the mixture to a bowl and let cool. Add the artichoke hearts, potatoes, cheese, and basil and mix well. Season with salt and pepper. Spread in the partially baked crust, top with the bread crumbs, and bake in the oven until golden brown, about 25 minutes. Remove from the oven and let cool for a few minutes. Slice and serve.

Harvest Stew
with Cheesy Dumplings

The cooking time for this vegetarian stew is about half that of a beef stew. **The dumplings make this a savory and filling dish. Serves 4**

2 tablespoons extra-virgin **olive oil**

1 large **onion**, diced

3 cloves **garlic**, minced

3 large **carrots**, peeled and diced

2 large **parsnips**, peeled and diced

3 ounces **button mushrooms**

2 unpeeled large **Yukon Gold potatoes**, diced

1 large **sweet potato**, peeled and diced

1 small **celeriac** (celery root), peeled and diced

6 cups **vegetable stock**

1 tablespoon **tomato paste**

2 teaspoons minced fresh **rosemary**

2 teaspoons minced fresh **oregano**

1 tablespoon minced fresh **thyme**

Salt and **cracked pepper** to taste

CHEESY DUMPLINGS

2 cups **all-purpose flour**

1 tablespoon **baking powder**

1 teaspoon **salt**

1 cup (4 ounces) shredded **sharp Cheddar cheese**

¼ cup **nonhydrogenated vegetable shortening**

1 cup **milk**

Preheat the oven to 400°F on Convection Bake. In a large ovenproof sauté pan or skillet, heat the oil over high heat until shimmering. Add the onion and sauté until it begins to brown, about 5 minutes. Add the garlic and sauté for 1 minute. Add the carrots, parsnips, mushrooms, potatoes, sweet potato, celeriac, stock, tomato paste, and herbs and bring to a boil. Season with salt and pepper. Cover and bake in the oven until the vegetables are tender, about 25 minutes.

While the vegetables are cooking, make the dumplings: In a large bowl, combine the flour, baking powder, and salt. Stir with a whisk to blend. Stir in the cheese. Add the shortening and rub in with your fingertips until the mixture resembles coarse meal. Add the milk and stir just until the batter comes together. Remove the stew from the oven. Taste and adjust the seasoning. Top the stew with large spoonfuls of the batter. Return to the oven and bake, uncovered, until the dumplings are golden brown, 10 to 12 minutes. Remove from the oven and serve.

Savannah's Favorite Four-Cheese Pasta

As the name might indicate, this is our daughter Savannah's most requested dinner; she would have it every night if we would let her. We always make extra sauce and freeze it for later use. Once you start making this sauce, you'll never go back to store-bought; in 20 minutes you can make the best little tomato sauce. **Serves 4**

MARINARA SAUCE

2 tablespoons
extra-virgin **olive oil**

6 cloves **garlic**, thinly sliced

Two 28-ounce cans finely
chopped tomatoes

1 tablespoon minced
fresh **basil**

2 teaspoons **dried oregano**

1 **bay leaf**

Salt and freshly ground
pepper to taste

16 large **pasta shells**

1 cup (8 ounces)
whole-milk ricotta

¾ cup (3 ounces) shredded
fontina cheese

¾ cup (3 ounces) shredded
mozzarella cheese

Salt and freshly ground
pepper to taste

½ cup (2 ounces) grated
Parmesan cheese

To make the sauce: In a large sauté pan or skillet, heat the oil over high heat until hot. Add the garlic and cook just until brown. (The garlic cooks quickly, so watch carefully.) Add the tomatoes, basil, oregano, and bay leaf. Reduce the heat to medium and cook for 20 minutes. In a blender, puree the sauce. Season with salt and pepper. Set aside.

Preheat the oven to 375°F on Convection Bake. Grease a 9-by-13-inch baking dish.

In a large pot of salted boiling water, cook the pasta until al dente, about 12 minutes. Drain. In a medium bowl, combine the ricotta, fontina, and mozzarella and mix well. Season with salt and pepper. Spoon into the cooked shells and place them in the prepared dish. Top the shells with the sauce and sprinkle with the Parmesan cheese. Bake in the oven until bubbling and golden brown, about 25 minutes. Let cool slightly, then serve.

Spinach-Fontina Lasagna

No-boil lasagna noodles have a tender texture, almost like fresh pasta, and **not having to boil the noodles saves you time and energy.** This is a filling and satisfying vegetarian dish.

Serves 6

WHITE SAUCE

5 cups **milk**

3 cloves **garlic**, minced

4 tablespoons unsalted **butter**, softened

¼ cup **all-purpose flour**

Salt and freshly ground **pepper** to taste

1 pound **spinach**, well rinsed and stemmed

4 cups (16 ounces) shredded **fontina cheese**

3 cups (24 ounces) **whole-milk ricotta**

Grated zest of 2 **lemons**

½ teaspoon **red pepper flakes**

One 8-ounce package no-boil **lasagna noodles**

1 cup fresh **bread crumbs**, toasted (see page 151)

To make the sauce: In a large saucepan, combine the milk and garlic and bring to a boil over high heat. While the milk is heating, mix the butter and flour together to form a soft dough. Gradually whisk the butter mixture into the boiling milk. Return to a boil, reduce the heat to a simmer, and cook for about 3 minutes, or until thickened. Strain through a fine-meshed sieve. Season with salt and pepper. Set aside.

Preheat the oven to 375°F on Convection Bake. Lightly grease a 9-by-13-inch baking dish.

In a large saucepan of salted boiling water, cook the spinach just until wilted, about 30 seconds. Drain and run cold water over the spinach to cool it. Squeeze as much water out of the spinach as possible and chop it finely. In a large bowl, combine the spinach, fontina, ricotta, lemon zest, and pepper flakes and mix well. Line the prepared baking dish with one layer of the noodles. Spread one-fourth of the sauce over the noodles, then top with about one-fourth of the spinach mixture. Repeat to make 3 more layers.

Top with the bread crumbs, cover with aluminum foil, and bake in the oven for 20 minutes. Remove the foil and bake for an additional 10 minutes, or until golden brown and bubbling. Remove from the oven and let stand for 10 minutes. Cut into squares and serve.

Bacon Mac and Cheese

Mac and cheese has been a family staple for many years. If you've never made it from scratch, you have no idea what you've been missing. Leave out the bacon for a vegetarian dish.

Serves 6

1 pound **elbow macaroni**

6 **slices bacon**, diced

3 cloves **garlic**, minced

1 cup **half-and-half**

1 cup **sour cream**

3 **eggs**

1 tablespoon **Dijon mustard**

2 teaspoons **Tabasco sauce**

1 cup (4 ounces) shredded **fontina cheese**

1 cup (4 ounces) shredded **Muenster cheese**

1 cup (4 ounces) shredded sharp **Cheddar cheese**

Salt and freshly ground **pepper** to taste

1½ cups fresh **bread crumbs**

¾ cup grated **Parmesan cheese**

Preheat the oven to 350°F on Convection Bake. Grease a 9-by-13-inch baking dish.

In a large pot of salted boiling water, cook the macaroni until al dente, about 6 minutes. Drain and rinse in cold water. Put the macaroni in a large bowl. In a small sauté pan over medium heat, cook the bacon until crisp. Drain on paper towels and set aside. In a small bowl, whisk together the garlic, half-and-half, sour cream, eggs, mustard, and Tabasco. Pour over the macaroni and mix well. Add the cheeses and mix well. Season with salt and pepper. Spread in the prepared baking dish.

In a small bowl, combine the bread crumbs and Parmesan. Stir to blend and sprinkle evenly over the macaroni. Bake in the oven until golden brown and bubbling, about 25 minutes. Remove from the oven and let cool slightly. Serve.

Wild Mushroom–Potato Cake

When this potato cake cooks, it fills the house with the most amazing smells of wild mushrooms and garlic. We also make this dish as a side dish for the holidays. **Serves 6**

8 **Yukon Gold potatoes**, peeled and diced

2 tablespoon unsalted **butter**

2 tablespoons extra-virgin **olive oil**

1 small **onion**, finely diced

4 cloves **garlic**, minced

12 ounces **mushrooms**, such as **shiitakes**, **morels**, and/or **chanterelles**, sliced

1 tablespoon minced fresh **thyme**

½ cup **dry sherry**

1 cup **sour cream**

½ cup **half-and-half**

2 cups (8 ounces) shredded **Gruyère cheese**

3 egg yolks

Salt and freshly ground **pepper** to taste

Preheat the oven to 375°F on Convection Bake. Grease a 9-inch springform pan. In a large pot of salted boiling water, cook the potatoes until tender, about 15 minutes. Meanwhile, in a large sauté pan or skillet, melt the butter with the oil over high heat. Add the onion and sauté for 2 minutes. Add the garlic and sauté for 2 minutes. Add the mushrooms and thyme; sauté until the mushrooms brown, about 8 minutes. Add the sherry and cook to reduce until dry, about 3 minutes.

Pour the mushroom mixture into a bowl and let cool. Drain the potatoes and add to the mushroom mixture. Add the sour cream, half-and-half, Gruyère, and egg yolks. Mash with a potato masher and season well with salt and pepper. Spoon into the prepared pan and smooth the top. Bake in the oven for 45 minutes, or until golden brown. Remove the sides from the pan. Cut the cake into wedges and serve.

BREAD IS ONE OF OUR FAVORITE FOODS TO MAKE AT HOME; NOTHING ELSE IS QUITE AS SATISFYING. OUR BREAD RECIPES ARE NOT THOSE OF PROFESSIONAL BAKERS, BUT OF TWO PEOPLE **WHO LOVE TO BAKE AND SHARE THEIR RECIPES WITH FAMILY AND FRIENDS**.

BREADS

Parmesan and Green Onion Biscuits

We love to make these quick little biscuits to go with stews and soups. Add a tossed green salad, and you have **the perfect cozy meal.** You can substitute other cheeses and herbs to vary the flavor of the biscuits. **Makes 12 biscuits**

3 cups **all-purpose flour**

1 tablespoon **baking powder**

1/2 cup grated **Parmesan cheese**

2 green **onions**, finely chopped, including green parts

2 teaspoons **salt**

1 cup (2 sticks) cold unsalted **butter**, diced, plus 2 tablespoons melted butter

1 cup **buttermilk**

Preheat the oven to 375°F on Convection Bake. Grease a baking sheet.

In a large bowl, combine the flour, baking powder, cheese, onions, and salt. Stir with a whisk to blend. Add the 1 cup butter and blend with your fingertips until the mixture resembles coarse meal. Add the buttermilk and stir with a fork just until the dough is moist. Transfer the dough to a lightly floured board and form into a rectangle about 1/2 inch thick. With a sharp knife, cut into 12 biscuits.

Place on the prepared pan and bake in the oven until golden brown, about 15 minutes. Remove from the oven, brush with melted butter, and serve hot.

Orange Spice Pecan Muffins

Depending on the time of year, **you can add blueberries or even chopped peaches to this recipe.** Make it without the topping and roll the warm muffins in melted butter, then in cinnamon sugar, to make what our family calls doughnut muffins. **Makes 12 muffins**

½ cup (1 stick) unsalted **butter**, softened

¾ cup **sugar**

2 large **eggs**

2 teaspoons **vanilla extract**

½ cup **milk**

2 cups **all-purpose flour**

2 teaspoons **baking powder**

¼ teaspoon **salt**

TOPPING

1 ¼ cups **pecans**, toasted (see page 151) and ground

Grated zest of 1 **orange**

¼ cup **sugar**

½ teaspoon ground **cinnamon**

¼ teaspoon ground **ginger**

¼ teaspoon ground **nutmeg**

Preheat the oven to 350°F on Convection Bake. Grease a 12-cup muffin pan.

In the bowl of a heavy-duty mixer fitted with the paddle attachment, cream the butter and sugar until light and fluffy, stopping to scrape down the sides and bottom of the bowl once or twice. Add the eggs, one at a time, and mix well after each addition. Add the vanilla and milk and mix well. In a medium bowl, combine the flour, baking powder, and salt. Stir with a whisk to blend. Add to the wet ingredients, mixing just until blended. Fill each muffin cup three-fourths full with batter.

To make the topping: In a medium bowl, combine all the topping ingredients and stir to blend. Sprinkle the topping evenly on each muffin.

Bake in the oven until the muffins are golden brown and slowly spring back when pressed gently, about 20 minutes. Remove from the oven and let cool for about 5 minutes. Unmold onto wire racks to cool completely. Serve.

Cappy's Weekday Bread

There is nothing like the smell and taste of homemade bread. **This quick weekday bread makes my family very happy.** I often triple the recipe and refrigerate the extra dough so I can bake a loaf after work. **Makes 1 loaf**

1 cup **warm water**
(105° to 115°F)

1 teaspoon **active dry yeast**

1 tablespoon extra-virgin
olive oil, plus oil for brushing

½ cup **whole-wheat flour**

About 2 cups **bread flour**

2 teaspoons **salt**

Sea salt for sprinkling

In the bowl of a heavy-duty mixer fitted with the dough hook, combine the water and yeast. Stir to dissolve the yeast; let stand until foamy, about 5 minutes. Add the 1 tablespoon olive oil, the whole-wheat flour, and 1 cup of the bread flour and mix well. With the machine running, add about ¼ cup of the bread flour at a time, mixing until the dough cleans the sides of the bowl. Add the 2 teaspoons salt and knead in the mixer for about 5 minutes.

On a lightly floured board, knead the dough until smooth and elastic, another 5 minutes. Form the dough into a ball and place in a well-oiled large resealable plastic bag. Seal and let rise at room temperature until doubled in volume, about 1 hour.

(Or to bake later, let the dough rise in the refrigerator for at least 24 hours or up to 3 days.)

Preheat the oven to 500°F on Convection Bake, with a baking stone inside, if you have one.

Remove the dough from the bag, place on a floured board, and form into a 6- or 7-inch round. Let rest for 20 minutes. Brush with olive oil and sprinkle with sea salt. Slide the bread onto the stone, if using, or bake on the baking sheet. Or, place the bread on a baking peel sprinkled with flour or a baking sheet lined with parchment paper. Bake until golden brown, 20 to 30 minutes. An instant-read thermometer inserted in the bread should register 200°F. Remove from the oven and let cool on a wire rack. Enjoy.

Bistro Challah Bread

We use this bread for sandwiches and even desserts at the bistro. **It's good for sandwiches and French toast,** or just toast it and enjoy with a bit of jam and butter. **Makes 2 loaves**

2 tablespoons **active dry yeast**

½ cup **sugar**

1 ¾ cups **warm water** (105° to 115°F)

½ cup (1 stick) unsalted **butter,** melted

4 large **eggs,** lightly beaten

5 to 6 cups **all-purpose flour**

1 tablespoon **salt**

Preheat the oven to 375°F on Convection Bake. Grease two 6-cup loaf pans.

In the bowl of a heavy-duty mixer fitted with the dough hook, combine the yeast, sugar, and water and mix well. Let stand until foamy, about 5 minutes. Add the butter and eggs and mix well. Add about 3 cups of the flour to the bowl and mix well. Add about ½ cup flour at a time to the dough, mixing well after each addition, until the dough cleans the sides of the bowl. Add the salt and mix for about 5 minutes.

On a lightly floured board, knead the dough until smooth and elastic, about 5 minutes. Form the dough into a ball and place in a well-oiled large resealable plastic bag. Seal and let rise at room temperature until doubled in volume, about 1 hour. (Or to bake later, let the dough rise in the refrigerator for at least 24 hours or up to 3 days.)

Gently remove from the bag and form into a 6-by-10-inch rectangle, then tightly roll into a cylinder. Cut the cylinder in half, and place each half in the prepared pans, seam side down. Bake until golden, about 1 hour. An instant-read thermometer inserted in the bread should read 200°F. Let cool in the pans for about 5 minutes, then unmold onto a wire rack to cool completely. Serve.

WE DON'T EAT A LOT OF DESSERTS AT OUR HOUSE, BUT WHEN WE DO, WE MAKE SURE IT'S A GOOD ONE. **WE LOVE DESSERTS THAT ARE DECADENT AND SOUL SATISFYING.** EVEN IF IT'S JUST SIMPLE CHOCOLATE-CHUNK COOKIES, WE USE THE BEST INGREDIENTS AND BAKE THEM WITH LOVE.

DESSERTS

Oven-Braised Pears
with Bittersweet Chocolate Sauce

So simple yet elegant, **this dessert can be dressed up** with ice cream instead of whipped cream and topped with shaved chocolate. It's a lovely finale for a company meal. **Serves 6**

4 cups **white wine**

¼ cup **amaretto liqueur**

1½ cups **sugar**

½ teaspoon **almond extract**

3 large **pears** such as Bartlett, peeled, cored, and halved

¾ cup **heavy cream**

Bittersweet Chocolate Sauce (recipe follows)

½ cup **sliced almonds**, toasted (see page 151)

Preheat the oven to 375°F on Convection Bake. In a large non-reactive sauté pan or skillet, combine the wine, liqueur, sugar, and almond extract. Bring to a boil over high heat. Add the pears and return to a boil. Cover and bake in the oven until tender, 15 to 20 minutes, depending on the ripeness of the pears.

In a deep bowl, whip the cream to soft peaks. Pool some of the chocolate sauce on each of 6 dessert plates. Top each with a pear half. Dollop each with whipped cream and sprinkle with the almonds. Serve.

Bittersweet Chocolate Sauce

Makes about 2 cups

½ cup (1 stick) unsalted **butter**, cut into pieces

1 cup **sugar**

1 cup **heavy cream**

⅓ cup **unsweetened cocoa powder**

Pinch of **salt**

1 tablespoon **vanilla extract**

In a medium saucepan, combine the butter, sugar, cream, and cocoa powder. Bring to a boil over medium heat, stirring frequently. Reduce the heat to low and simmer for 4 to 5 minutes, or until the sauce coats the back of a spoon. Remove from the heat and stir in the salt and vanilla. Serve warm or at room temperature.

Roasted Peaches
with Caramel Ganache

I thought of this ganache recipe one night when I couldn't sleep, and it worked so well that we have used it on everything from pumpkin pie to fresh berries. **It's perfect paired with oven-roasted peaches.** Serves 4

CARAMEL GANACHE

½ cup **sugar**

¼ cup **water**

1 cup **heavy cream**

¼ teaspoon **sea salt**

2 unpeeled **peaches**, halved and pitted

½ cup **sugar**

¼ cup **dry white wine**

½ teaspoon **vanilla extract**

To make the ganache: In a sauté pan or skillet, place the sugar and carefully moisten it with the water without splashing. Cook over high heat without stirring until the sugar starts to color. Swirl to even the color and cook until golden brown. Carefully pour in the cream and cook until the mixture forms a sauce. Add the salt. Remove from the heat and refrigerate until cold.

Preheat the oven to 425°F on Convection Bake. In a medium non-reactive ovenproof sauté pan or skillet, combine the peaches, sugar, wine, and vanilla. Bake in the oven until tender, 20 to 25 minutes. Remove from the oven and let cool slightly. While the peaches are cooling, whip the ganache until soft peaks form; do not overwhip.

To serve, divide the peaches among shallow bowls with some of the cooking liquid. Top with the whipped ganache and serve.

Butternut Squash Tart
with Pecan Crust

We came up with this recipe as a substitute for pumpkin pie for our Thanksgiving cooking class. **It's sophisticated, yet familiar enough to be a crowd pleaser** for the holidays. Other winter squash, such as Hubbard or acorn, can be substituted for the butternut squash.

Makes one 9-inch tart; serves 10

1½–2 pounds **butternut squash**

PECAN CRUST

2¼ cups **pecans**, lightly toasted (see page 151)

6 tablespoons unsalted **butter**

¼ cup **sugar**

Pinch of **salt**

1 cup (8 ounces) **cream cheese**

1 cup **sugar**

3 **eggs**, lightly beaten

½ teaspoon ground **cinnamon**

½ teaspoon ground **allspice**

Pinch of ground **nutmeg**

Pinch of ground **cloves**

1 teaspoon **vanilla extract**

Pinch of **salt**

Softly **whipped cream** for serving

Preheat the oven to 350°F on Convection Bake. Grease a 9-inch tart pan with a removable bottom.

Cut the squash in half and scoop out the seeds. Place, cut sides down, in a roasting pan. Bake in the oven until tender, about 45 minutes. Remove from the oven and scoop the pulp into a small bowl. Let cool.

To make the crust: In a food processor, pulse the nuts until ground. Add the butter, sugar, and salt and pulse until mixed well. Press into the bottom and up the sides of the prepared pan. Refrigerate for at least 30 minutes.

In a food processor, combine 1½ cups of the squash, the cream cheese, and sugar. Process until smooth. With the machine running, add the eggs one at a time. Add the spices, vanilla, and salt and mix well. Pour into the prepared crust and bake in the oven just until set, 35 to 40 minutes. Remove from the oven and let cool slightly. Serve warm, with softly whipped cream.

Fromage Blanc – Brown Sugar Tart

Fromage blanc is a soft fresh cheese made with either cow's or goat's milk. The cheese made with cow's milk is milder in flavor, so **it is better for desserts.** **Makes one 10-inch tart; serves 10**

BROWN SUGAR CRUST

2 cups **all-purpose flour**

½ cup **brown sugar**

½ teaspoon **vanilla extract**

½ teaspoon **salt**

1 cup (2 sticks) cold **unsalted butter**, cut into pieces

FILLING

1 cup (8 ounces) **fromage blanc cheese**

1 cup **heavy cream**

½ **cup sugar**

4 **eggs**

Pinch of ground **nutmeg**

Pinch of ground **ginger**

Pinch of ground **cinnamon**

½ teaspoon **vanilla extract**

Softly **whipped cream** for serving

Preheat the oven to 375°F on Convection Bake. Grease a 10-inch tart pan with a removeable bottom.

To make the crust: In a food processor, combine the flour, sugar, vanilla, and salt and process to mix. With the machine running, add the butter one piece at a time. Process until a ball of dough rides on top of the blades. Remove the dough and press it evenly over the bottom and up the sides of the prepared pan. Bake in the oven just until set, about 10 minutes. Remove from the oven and let cool. Reduce the oven temperature to 325°F.

To make the filling: In a medium bowl, combine the cheese, cream, and sugar. Whisk until smooth. Whisk in the eggs, spices, and vanilla. Pour into the prepared crust. Bake in the oven for 20 minutes, or until the custard is just set. Remove from the oven and let cool slightly. Serve warm, with softly whipped cream.

Apple and Sour Cherry Pie

We love the tart little bites of flavor the dried cherries add to this pie. If you don't want to use wine to soak the cherries, water is a fine substitute.

Makes one 9-inch tart; serves 10

1 cup **dried sour** (tart) **cherries**

1 cup **red wine** or **port**

2 recipes **Cappy's Pie Dough** (page 149)

6 tart **baking apples**, such as Granny Smiths, peeled, cored, and cut into ¼-inch-thick slices

1 cup **sugar**, plus 2 tablespoons

3 tablespoons **all-purpose flour**

2½ teaspoons ground **cinnamon**

½ teaspoon ground **nutmeg**

¼ teaspoon ground **ginger**

1 tablespoon unsalted **butter**

2 tablespoons **milk**

Vanilla ice cream for serving

Preheat the oven to 375°F on Convection Bake. In a medium saucepan, combine the cherries and wine or port. Bring to a boil over high heat. Reduce the heat to medium and simmer until the cherries are plump and have absorbed most of the liquid, about 5 minutes.

On a well-floured board, roll out one dough disc to an 11-inch round. Fit into a 9-inch pie plate. Trim the edges to a ½-inch overhang. In a large bowl, combine the apples, the 1 cup sugar, flour, spices, and cherries. Toss well. Pour into the prepared crust and dot with the butter. Roll the second dough disc out to an 11-inch round. Place on top of the filling and trim the edges to a 1-inch overhang. Fold the edges of the top crust under the edges of the bottom crust and flute. Brush the crust with the milk and dust with the 2 tablespoons sugar.

Bake in the oven for 15 minutes, then reduce the oven temperature to 350°F. Bake 45 minutes longer, or until golden brown and bubbling. Remove from the oven and let cool for 20 minutes. Serve warm, with vanilla ice cream.

French Apple Tart

This tart has two layers of apples: a simple applesauce, topped with sliced apples to enhance the texture. Gravenstein apples work best for this tart, but the season is short, and Granny Smiths will work when Gravensteins aren't available.

Makes one 9-inch tart; serves 10

Cappy's Pie Dough (page 149)

6 **Gravenstein** or
Granny Smith apples,
peeled and cored

2 tablespoons unsalted **butter**

¾ cup **sugar**

1 teaspoon **vanilla extract**

Grated zest of 1 **lemon**

¼ teaspoon freshly
grated nutmeg

Pinch of **salt**

Softly **whipped cream** or
vanilla ice cream for serving

Preheat the oven to 375°F on Convection Bake. Grease a 9-inch tart pan with a removable bottom.

On a well-floured board, roll the dough out to an 11-inch round. Fit into the prepared pan and trim the edges. Refrigerate until ready to use.

Dice 3 of the apples and cut the other 3 into thin slices. In a medium sauté pan or skillet, melt the butter over medium heat and add the diced apples, ½ cup of the sugar, the vanilla, lemon zest, nutmeg, and salt. Cook until the apples are tender, about 4 minutes. Let cool slightly, then spread in the prepared crust. Overlap the sliced apples in concentric circles on top of the cooked apples. Sprinkle with the remaining ¼ cup of sugar. Bake in the oven until the apples are golden brown, about 35 minutes. Remove from the oven and let cool slightly. Serve warm, with softly whipped cream or vanilla ice cream.

Raspberry Galette *with* Lemon Topping

You can use just about any seasonal fruit for this tart, but if using a less-juicy fruit such as apples or pears, cut the cornstarch to ½ cup. **Makes one 9-inch galette; serves 10**

Cappy's Pie Dough (page 149)

FILLING

4 cups fresh **raspberries**

½ cup **sugar**

⅓ cup **cornstarch**

1 teaspoon **vanilla extract**

½ teaspoon ground **ginger**

TOPPING

½ cup **all-purpose flour**

½ cup **sugar**

⅓ cup unsalted **butter**, softened

Grated zest of 1 **lemon**

Pinch of **salt**

Softly **whipped cream** or **vanilla ice cream** for serving

Preheat the oven to 400°F on Convection Bake. Grease a baking sheet.

On a well-floured board, roll the dough out to a 10-inch round. Place the dough on the prepared pan.

To make the filling: In a large bowl, combine all of the filling ingredients. Pile the berry mixture in the center of the dough and fold 1 inch of the dough over the berries.

To make the topping: In a medium bowl, combine all of the topping ingredients and mix with your fingers to form a coarse meal. Sprinkle over the berries. Bake in the oven until the crust is golden brown and the berries are bubbling, about 1 hour. Remove from the oven and let cool slightly. Serve warm, with softly whipped cream or vanilla ice cream.

Strawberry-Rhubarb Cobbler

When making the biscuit topping for this cobbler, don't over-work the dough, so the topping will be tender. **Change the fruit with the seasons,** trying different combinations as the mood strikes you. **Serves 10**

3 cups finely diced **rhubarb**

5 cups fresh **strawberries**, sliced

1 cup **sugar**

1 teaspoon **vanilla extract**

¼ cup **all-purpose flour**

TOPPING

2 cups **all-purpose flour**

1 tablespoon **baking powder**

½ teaspoon **salt**

¾ cup (1 ½ sticks) cold unsalted **butter**, diced

1 cup **milk**

1 tablespoon **sugar**

½ teaspoon ground **cinnamon**

Softly **whipped cream** or **vanilla ice cream** for serving

Preheat the oven to 350°F on Convection Bake. In a large bowl, combine the rhubarb, berries, and sugar. Mix well. Add the vanilla and flour and gently toss to coat. Spread in an 8-cup baking dish.

To make the topping: In a large bowl, combine the flour, baking powder, and salt. Stir with a whisk to blend. Add the butter and rub it in with your fingertips until the mixture resembles coarse meal. Stir in the milk and mix just until the dough comes together; do not overmix. Drop spoonfuls of the dough on top of the berry mixture, covering the entire top of the cobbler. Mix the sugar and cinnamon together in a small bowl. Sprinkle on top of the dough. Bake in the oven until golden brown and bubbling, about 50 minutes. Remove from the oven and serve with softly whipped cream or vanilla ice cream.

Cappy's Sugar Cookies

These are our son Alex's favorite cookies, and if I am in a hurry I can have them ready to chill in about 10 minutes. They will keep frozen for about 6 months. Add cinnamon, orange zest, or spices to the dough to flavor the cookies according to your mood.

Makes about 30 cookies

2 cups **all-purpose flour**

3/4 cup **sugar**, plus 1/2 cup

1/2 teaspoon **salt**

1 teaspoon **vanilla extract**

1 cup (2 sticks) unsalted **butter**, softened

Preheat the oven to 350°F on Convection Bake. Grease a baking sheet.

In the bowl of a food processor, combine the flour, the 3/4 cup sugar, the salt, and vanilla and process to blend. With the machine running, add the butter 1 tablespoon at a time. Process until the dough rides on top of the blades. Spread the 1/2 cup sugar on a work surface and transfer the dough to the sugar. Roll the dough into an 18-inch-long cylinder. Wrap in plastic and refrigerate for at least 30 minutes or up to 2 days.

Cut into 1/4-inch slices and place 1 inch apart on the prepared pan. Bake in the oven until golden brown, about 12 minutes. Let cool on the pan for about 3 minutes, then transfer to wire racks to cool completely. Store in an airtight container for up to 1 week.

Coconut-Orange Cookies

The cornstarch in the recipe **helps make crisp cookies.** Try adding lime zest or even grapefruit zest to the cookies instead of orange. The dough freezes well, for up to 6 months. **Makes 36 cookies**

1 ³/₄ cups **all-purpose flour**

½ cup **cornstarch**

1 teaspoon **baking powder**

½ teaspoon **salt**

1 cup (2 sticks) unsalted **butter**, softened

1 cup **sugar**

1 large **egg**

Grated zest of 1 **orange**

½ teaspoon **orange oil** (optional)

1 teaspoon **vanilla extract**

1⅓ cups **sweetened shredded coconut**, lightly toasted (see page 151)

Preheat the oven to 350°F on Convection Bake. Grease 2 baking sheets. In a medium bowl, combine the flour, cornstarch, baking powder, and salt. Stir with a whisk to blend.

In the bowl of a heavy-duty mixer fitted with the paddle attachment, cream the butter and sugar on medium speed until light and fluffy. Add the egg, orange zest, oil, and vanilla and mix well. Gradually add the dry ingredients and mix well, stopping once or twice to scrape the sides and bottom of the bowl. Add the coconut and mix well. Cover and refrigerate for at least 30 minutes.

Using a small ice cream scoop or a teaspoon, place small scoops of batter about 2 inches apart on a baking sheet and gently press each to flatten slightly. Bake in the oven for about 10 minutes, or until light brown. Let cool on the pan for 3 minutes, then transfer the cookies to wire racks to cool completely. Store in an airtight container for up to 1 week.

Chocolate Chunk Cookies

You can make these cookies with good-quality chocolate chips, but we **love the chopped chocolate** because it isn't uniform in size. Use different nuts, if you like, and consider adding some dried cherries as well. **Makes about 24 cookies**

1 cup (2 sticks) unsalted **butter**, melted and cooled

1 cup **granulated sugar**

½ cup **brown sugar**

2 **eggs**

1 teaspoon **vanilla extract**

2¼ cups **all-purpose flour**

½ teaspoon **baking soda**

½ teaspoon **salt**

½ cup **hazelnuts**, toasted and skinned (see page 151)

12 ounces **bittersweet chocolate**, chopped

Preheat the oven to 300°F on Convection Bake. Grease 2 baking sheets.

In a large bowl, combine the butter, granulated sugar, and brown sugar. Mix well. Add the eggs and vanilla and mix until smooth. In a medium bowl, combine the flour, baking soda, and salt. Stir with a whisk to blend. Add to the wet ingredients and stir until smooth. Fold in the nuts and chocolate.

Spoon heaping tablespoons of dough about 1 inch apart on the prepared pans. Bake until golden brown, about 12 minutes. Remove from the oven and let cool on the pans for 3 minutes, then transfer to wire racks to finish cooling. Store in an airtight container for up to 1 week.

Coconut-Cashew Brownies

3/4 cup (1 1/2 sticks) unsalted **butter**

5 ounces **bittersweet chocolate**, minced

1 cup **brown sugar**

1/2 cup **granulated sugar**

3 **eggs**, lightly beaten

2 tablespoons **dark rum**

1 teaspoon **vanilla extract**

1/2 cup **all-purpose flour**

1/2 teaspoon **salt**

1 cup finely chopped **roasted cashews**

1/2 cup **coconut**, lightly toasted (see page 151)

1/3 cup **cacao nibs**

If you want to make this recipe fancier, divide the batter among 6 lightly greased 8-ounce ramekins. Bake at the same temperature just until set, and **serve warm, topped with whipped cream or ice cream.** **Makes 16 brownies**

Preheat the oven to 325°F on Convection Bake. Grease an 8-inch square pan.

In a medium stainless-steel bowl, combine the butter and chocolate. Set the bowl over a saucepan of simmering water. Melt the chocolate halfway, then turn the heat off and let sit until completely melted. Stir until smooth, add the sugars, and mix well. Stir in the eggs, rum, and vanilla.

In a medium bowl, combine the flour, salt, nuts, coconut, and nibs. Stir to blend, then gradually stir into the wet ingredients. Pour into the prepared pan. Bake in the oven just until set, about 20 minutes. The brownies are done when a knife inserted in the center comes out moist. Do not over-bake. Let cool and cut into squares.

Oatmeal–Peanut Brittle Bars

The peanut brittle in this recipe adds a layer of crunchy texture. Use good-quality peanut brittle or even almond brittle. **Makes about 30 bars**

1 cup (2 sticks) unsalted **butter,** melted

1 cup **granulated sugar**

½ cup **brown sugar**

1 **egg**

³/₄ cups **all-purpose flour**

2 ½ cups **old-fashioned rolled oats**

½ teaspoon ground **cinnamon**

1 teaspoon **vanilla extract**

½ teaspoon **salt**

³/₄ cup finely chopped **peanut brittle**

2 cups (12 ounces) **chocolate chips**

Preheat the oven to 350°F on Convection Bake. Grease an 11-x-17-inch rimmed baking sheet.

In the bowl of a heavy-duty mixer fitted with the paddle attachment, combine the butter and sugars. Mix on medium speed until smooth. Beat in the egg. In a medium bowl, combine the flour, oats, cinnamon, vanilla, and salt. Remove the egg mixture from the machine and fold in the peanut brittle and chocolate chips. Press the cookie dough evenly into the prepared pan; the dough will be very thin.

Bake in the oven until golden brown, about 20 minutes. Let cool for about 3 minutes, then cut into about 30 squares. Let cool completely, then remove from the pan using a metal spatula. Store in an airtight container for up to 1 week.

Cinnamon Graham Crackers

Homemade graham crackers are a special treat—they aren't too sweet, and **the graham flour is a nutritious whole-grain ingredient.** You won't feel guilty giving your kids this cookie after school. **Makes about 30 crackers**

¾ cup (1 ½ sticks) unsalted **butter**, softened

¾ cup **brown sugar**

1 teaspoon **vanilla extract**

½ cup **half-and-half**

2 cups **graham flour**

1 cup **all-purpose flour**

1 teaspoon **baking powder**

½ teaspoon **baking soda**

½ teaspoon **salt**

½ cup **superfine sugar** mixed with 1 teaspoon ground **cinnamon**

Preheat the oven to 350°F on Convection Bake. Lightly grease a baking sheet.

In a heavy-duty mixer fitted with the paddle attachment, cream the butter, brown sugar, and vanilla until very light and fluffy. Mix in the half-and-half until smooth. In a medium bowl, combine the graham flour, all-purpose flour, baking powder, baking soda, and salt. Stir with a whisk to blend. On low speed, gradually add the dry ingredients to the wet ingredients, stopping to scrape the sides and bottom of the bowl once or twice.

On a lightly floured board, form the dough into a disc. Wrap in plastic and refrigerate for 30 minutes.

Roll the dough out on a lightly floured board to a ¼-inch thickness. With a 1-inch cookie cutter, cut out the cookies and sprinkle them liberally with the cinnamon sugar. Place on the prepared pan. Bake for about 12 minutes, or until golden brown. Let cool on the pan for 3 minutes, then transfer the cookies to a wire rack to cool completely. Store in an airtight container for up to 1 week.

Warm Mascarpone Cheesecakes

Like many good things, this dessert was an accident. Once, when we were teaching a class, we didn't have time to chill the cheesecakes. The result was a **warm cheesecakes with an almost puddinglike texture.** These can also be served at room temperature or cold, which makes them ideal for any dinner party. Garnish with berries for a festive touch.

Makes 8 individual cheesecakes

1 pound **cream cheese**, softened

2 cups (1 pound) **mascarpone cheese**

1¼ cups **sugar**

1 teaspoon **vanilla extract**

Grated zest of 1 **lemon**

5 large **eggs**

Pinch of **salt**

Softly **whipped cream** for serving

Preheat the oven to 275°F on Convection Bake. In a food processor, process the cream cheese until smooth. Add the mascarpone and sugar and mix until smooth. Add the vanilla and lemon zest and mix well. Add the eggs and salt and process until very smooth. Divide the batter among eight 8-ounce ramekins and place them in a roasting pan. Fill the pan with hot water to halfway up the sides of the ramekins. Bake for about 40 minutes, or until just set. Let cool for 10 to 15 minutes, then serve warm, with the softly whipped cream.

Almond Pound Cake

Pound cakes are so versatile. You can serve them plain, frost and fill them, or **top slices with fresh berries or chocolate sauce.** Vary the flavor of this cake by adding grated orange or lemon zest. **Makes 1 cake; serves 8**

½ cup (1 stick) unsalted **butter**, softened

1½ cups **sugar**

⅓ cup **almond paste**

½ teaspoon **vanilla extract**

½ teaspoon **almond extract**

4 **eggs**

½ cup **sour cream**

2 cups **all-purpose flour**

1 teaspoon **baking powder**

¼ teaspoon **baking soda**

Pinch of **salt**

Preheat the oven to 325°F on Convection Bake. Grease a 10-inch Bundt pan. In the bowl of a heavy-duty mixer fitted with the paddle attachment, combine the butter, sugar, almond paste, vanilla, and almond extract. Cream the mixture until light and fluffy, stopping once or twice to scrape the sides and bottom of the bowl. Add the eggs, one at a time, mixing well after each addition. Add the sour cream and mix well. In a medium bowl, combine the flour, baking powder, soda, and salt. Stir with a whisk to blend. Add the dry ingredients to the wet ingredients and mix just until smooth.

Pour the batter into the prepared pan and bake in the oven until the cake slowly springs back when pressed gently in the center, about 1 hour. Let cool in the pan for about 10 minutes, then unmold onto a wire rack to cool completely. Cut into slices to serve.

Individual Ginger-Chocolate Cakes

These cakes can be served warm or at room temperature, **making them the perfect party treat.** In summer, we add fresh berries as a garnish.

Makes 8 individual cakes

5 ounces **unsweetened chocolate**, chopped

½ cup (1 stick) cold unsalted **butter**, diced

1 ½ cups **sugar**

4 large **eggs**

1 teaspoon **vanilla extract**

½ cup **all-purpose flour**

¼ teaspoon ground **ginger**

4 ounces **bittersweet chocolate**, chopped

1 tablespoon minced **candied ginger**

Ice cream or **whipped cream** for serving

Preheat the oven to 325°F on Convection Bake. Grease eight 6-ounce ramekins.

In a double boiler over barely simmering water, melt the chocolate and butter; stir to blend. Let cool slightly.

In a medium bowl, combine the sugar, eggs, and vanilla. Beat until blended. Stir in the flour and ground ginger and mix well. Fold in the chocolate mixture, the chopped bittersweet chocolate, and candied ginger.

Spoon the batter into the prepared ramekins. Place on a baking sheet and bake in the oven just until set, 20 to 25 minutes. Remove from the oven and let cool slightly. Serve warm, with ice cream or whipped cream.

Rocky Road Cupcakes

This is a variation on a cake recipe from my friend Melissa Cary, by way of her friend Michelle Dennis. **These rich cupcakes are the best. Makes 36 cupcakes**

3 cups **all-purpose flour**

2½ cups **sugar**

1 cup **unsweetened cocoa powder**

1½ teaspoons **baking soda**

½ teaspoon **salt**

3 **eggs**

1⅓ cups **canola oil**

1½ cups **buttermilk**

1½ cups hot strongly **brewed coffee**

2 teaspoons **vanilla extract**

6 ounces **bittersweet chocolate**, chopped

3 cups **mini marshmallows**

1 cup blanched **almonds**, toasted (see page 151) and chopped

FROSTING

1 cup (2 sticks) unsalted **butter,** softened

3 tablespoons **unsweetened cocoa powder**

2 teaspoons **vanilla extract**

3 cups **confectioners' sugar**

36 **mini marshmallows** for garnish

Preheat the oven to 325°F on Convection Bake. Grease a 12-cup muffin pan and line the cups with baking papers.

In the bowl of a heavy-duty mixer fitted with a paddle attachment, combine the flour, sugar, cocoa powder, baking soda, and salt. Mix well. In a medium bowl, whisk the eggs, oil, buttermilk, coffee, and vanilla together. Gradually add the wet ingredients to the dry and mix well, stopping to scrape the sides and bottom of the bowl once or twice. Remove from the mixer and fold in the chocolate, marshmallows, and nuts by hand.

Fill the prepared muffin cups to just below the top, making sure each cupcake has enough solids. Bake in the oven for 15 minutes, or until a knife inserted in the center of a cupcake comes out moist. Remove from the oven and let cool in the pan for 10 minutes. Unmold and let cool completely.

To make the frosting: In the bowl of a heavy-duty mixer fitted with the paddle attachment, beat the butter and cocoa on medium speed until very soft and creamy. Add the vanilla, then gradually add the sugar ½ cup at a time. Mix until very smooth and creamy. Remove from the mixer and frost the cupcakes. Garnish each cupcake with a mini marshmallow.

THIS CHAPTER CONTAINS BASIC RECIPES AND TECHNIQUES NEEDED TO PREPARE SOME OF THE RECIPES IN THIS BOOK. **THE SIMPLE RECIPES FOR ACCOMPANIMENTS** SUCH AS CONVECTION-BAKED TORTILLAS AND PITA CHIPS **WILL APPEAL TO FIRST-TIME COOKS AND EXPERIENCED HOME CHEFS ALIKE**.

BASICS

Pizza Dough

Pizza is a family favorite, so we make a double batch of dough, then freeze half for another night. The dough can be frozen for up to 6 months.

Makes dough for two 12-inch pizzas

1 ½ teaspoons active dry **yeast**

1 ½ cups warm **water** (105° to 115°F)

2 tablespoons extra-virgin **olive oil**

About 2 ¾ cups **bread flour**

2 teaspoons **salt**

To make by machine: In the bowl of a heavy-duty mixer fitted with the dough hook, sprinkle the yeast over the water and stir to dissolve. Let stand for 5 minutes, or until foamy. Add the olive oil and 1 cup of the flour and mix on medium speed. With the machine running, add about ½ cup of the flour at a time until the dough cleans the sides of the bowl but sticks to the bottom. Add the salt and knead for 5 minutes on medium speed until the dough is smooth.

On a lightly floured board, knead the dough by hand for about 5 minutes, or until shiny and elastic.

To make by hand: In a medium bowl, combine the yeast and water and mix to dissolve. Let stand for 5 minutes, or until foamy. Add the olive oil and 1 cup of the flour and mix well. Add about ½ cup of flour at a time until the dough cleans the sides of the bowl but sticks to the bottom. Add the salt and mix until the dough is smooth. On a lightly floured board, knead the dough for 10 minutes, or until shiny and elastic.

Form into a ball and put into a well-oiled large plastic bag. Let rise at room temperature for about 1 hour, or until doubled in volume.

Crostini

Crostini is just a fancy name for toasts; use your leftover bread and simply bake with some good-quality olive oil. Use these little toasts for bruschetta, dips, or to float in a wonderful soup.

Makes 2 dozen toasts

24 slices good-quality **baguette**

2 tablespoons extra-virgin **olive oil**

2 cloves **garlic**

Preheat the oven to 375°F on Convection Bake. Place the bread on a baking sheet and drizzle with the olive oil. Bake until golden brown, 10 to 12 minutes. Remove from the oven and rub each piece of bread with garlic. Store in an airtight container for up to 2 days.

Cappy's Pie Dough

Makes enough dough for an 8- or 9-inch single crust

1 ⅓ cups **all-purpose flour**

½ teaspoon **salt**

⅓ cup cold unsalted **butter**, diced

⅓ cup cold nonhydrogenated **vegetable shortening**

5 tablespoons cold **water**

In a medium bowl, combine the flour and salt and stir with a whisk to blend. Add the butter and shortening and rub them in with your fingertips until the mixture resembles coarse meal. Gradually add the water, carefully mixing with a fork just until the dough is moistened. On a lightly floured board, form the dough into a disc. Cover with plastic wrap and refrigerate for 30 minutes before using.

Herbed Croutons

Makes 4 cups

4 cups diced good-quality stale **bread**

3 tablespoons extra-virgin **olive oil**

2 cloves **garlic**, minced

1 teaspoon minced fresh **basil**

1 teaspoon minced fresh **thyme**

1 teaspoon minced fresh flat-leaf **parsley**

½ cup (2 ounces) grated **Parmesan cheese**

Preheat the oven to 375°F on Convection Bake. In a large bowl, drizzle the bread with the olive oil and toss well. Add the garlic, herbs, and cheese. Toss to coat. Place on a rimmed baking sheet. Bake in the oven for 10 minutes. Stir well, then bake for another 10 minutes, or until golden brown. Remove from the oven and let cool. Store in an airtight container for up to 2 days.

Pita Chips

Makes 30 chips

3 **pita breads**, each cut into 5 wedges, then split in two

3 tablespoons extra-virgin **olive oil**

Sea salt to taste

Preheat the oven to 375°F on Convection Bake. Spread the pita slices on 2 rimmed baking sheets. Drizzle with the olive oil and sprinkle with salt. Bake in the oven until golden brown, 12 to 14 minutes. Remove and let cool. Store in an airtight container for up to 3 days.

Baked Tortillas

Makes 24

4 large **flour tortillas**, each cut into 6 wedges

2 tablespoons extra-virgin **olive oil**

Sea salt to taste

Preheat the oven to 375°F on Convection Bake. Spread the tortillas on a rimmed baking sheet. Drizzle with the olive oil and sprinkle with salt. Bake in the oven until golden brown, 12 to 14 minutes. Remove from the oven and let cool. Store in an airtight container for up to 3 days.

Toasting Nuts

Preheat the oven to 350°F on Convection Bake.
Place the nuts on a rimmed baking sheet and bake in the oven until golden brown, 10 to 12 minutes, depending on the nut. Let cool.

Toasting and Skinning Hazelnuts

Preheat the oven to 350°F on Convection Bake.
Spread the hazelnuts on a rimmed baking sheet and bake in the oven until the skins start to blister, about 15 minutes. Let cool, then rub between your hands to remove as many of the skins as possible.

Toasting Coconut

Preheat the oven to 350°F on Convection Bake.
Spread the coconut on a rimmed baking sheet and bake in the oven for 5 minutes. Stir well. Bake for another 5 minutes, or until golden brown. Let cool.

Toasting Bread Crumbs

Preheat the oven to 350°F on Convection Bake.
Spread the bread crumbs on a rimmed baking sheet. Bake in the oven for 4 minutes. Stir well. Bake for another 4 to 5 minutes, or until golden brown. Let cool.

Trimming Artichokes

Trim off about 1/2 inch of the top of the artichoke with a very sharp knife. Trim off the stem.

Roasting Peppers and Chilies

Preheat the oven on high on Convection Broil.
Place the peppers or chilies on a broiler pan and place under the broiler about 4 inches from the heat source. Turn to blacken on all sides, about 10 to 12 minutes for large peppers or chilies and 6 to 8 minutes for small ones.

Ingredient Glossary

ANCHO CHILI: A reddish brown dried chili with a mild spicy flavor.

ANCHO CHILI POWDER: A pure chili powder made from ancho chilies.

ASIAN SESAME OIL: An intensely flavored dark oil made from toasted sesame seeds.

BASMATI RICE: A long-grain rice with a nutlike flavor and aroma.

CACAO NIBS: The chopped, peeled, and shelled seeds of cacao beans.

CAYENNE SAUCE: A hot sauce made from cayenne chilies, vinegar. and salt. Milder than Tabasco sauce, it also has a more pronounced vinegar flavor.

CHINESE DRY MUSTARD: A powdered mustard, traditionally mixed with water and soy sauce to form a paste. English dry mustard may be substituted.

FISH SAUCE: A pungent Southeast Asian sauce made from salted and fermented fish.

FROMAGE BLANC: A fresh white cheese made with cow's or goat's milk.

GRAHAM FLOUR: A whole-wheat flour with a slightly coarser grain than regular whole-wheat flour.

GREEK YOGURT: A thick, velvety yogurt made from cow's milk.

HERBES DE PROVENCE: A traditional blend of herbs from the South of France, usually including thyme, rosemary, summer savory, lavender, sage, marjoram, and fennel seeds.

JASMINE RICE: An aromatic rice, originally from Thailand.

MASCARPONE CHEESE: A triple-cream cheese from the Lombardy region of Italy.

MIRIN: A sweet Japanese rice wine.

NONHYDROGENATED VEGETABLE SHORTENING: A solid shortening made from palm oil, available in tubs in natural foods stores and many supermarkets.

QUESO FRESCO: A slightly salty fresh white Mexican cheese, with a texture similar to farmer's cheese.

SRIRACHA SAUCE: A very hot, spicy Thai chili sauce used as a dipping sauce.

SWEET CHILI SAUCE: A thick, sweet chili sauce from Thailand, traditionally used on barbecued chicken.

SWEET SOY: A thick, sweet Indonesian sauce that is slightly less salty than regular soy sauce.

SWEET SPANISH SMOKED PAPRIKA (PIMENTÓN): A sweet, dark red paprika with a smoky flavor, made from peppers that have been smoked over a wood fire.

THAI GREEN CURRY PASTE: A thick, spicy sauce, usually made with onions, green chilies, fresh cilantro, lime zest, garlic, and fresh ginger or galangal. It can be found in the Asian section of specialty foods stores and some supermarkets.

Index